"This book is a game changer! I have put it on my 'must-read' list for my teen clients, their parents, and for any therapist working with individuals with OCD. This gem of a book is engaging, easy-to-read, and contains essential research-based tools to help teens recognize how to use their own strength, values, and their power of choice as weapons against the pain and suffering caused by OCD. I love that it can be used by teens and their families on its own or as a companion guide to use with a therapist."

—*Dr. Allison Solomon, Psy.D., licensed psychologist,*
Director and Founder of The Virtual Center for Anxiety & OCD

"This book should be on every OCD therapists' shelf! This workbook is such a wonderful addition for anyone trying to help a teen with OCD. It provides a simple and engaging way to view OCD, and offers concrete ways to work on it. It is definitely a book I will be recommending!"

—*Natasha Daniels, LCSW, child and teen OCD therapist,*
and author of Anxiety Sucks! A Teen Survival Guide

"Dr. Z.'s teen-friendly workbook introduces the reader to OCD, ACT, Choice Points, and a large toolbox of skills through cartoon illustrations, diagrams, case presentations, quizzes, games, and exercises. Engaging and informative, teens will find this workbook helpful in learning to better manage their OCD symptoms."

—*Allen H. Weg, Ed.D., Founder and Director of Stress and*
Anxiety Services of New Jersey, President, OCD New Jersey,
and author of OCD Treatment Through Storytelling

T0301131

of related interest

Stand Up to OCD!
A CBT Self-Help Guide and Workbook for Teens
Kelly Wood and Douglas Fletcher
ISBN 978 1 78592 835 2
eISBN 978 1 78450 973 6

The Mental Health and Wellbeing Workout for Teens
Skills and Exercises from ACT and CBT for Healthy Thinking
Paula Nagel
Illustrated by Gary Bainbridge
ISBN 978 1 78592 394 4
eISBN 978 1 78450 753 4

Obsessive Compulsive Disorder Diary
A Self-Help Diary with CBT Activities to Challenge Your OCD
Charlotte Dennis
Foreword by Dr Amita Jassi and Dr Zoe Kindynis, National & Specialist
OCD, BDD and Related Disorders Clinic, Maudsley Hospital
ISBN 978 1 78775 053 1
eISBN 978 1 78775 054 8

Breaking Free from OCD
A CBT Guide for Young People and Their Families
Jo Derisley, Isobel Heyman, Sarah Robinson and Cynthia Turner
ISBN 978 1 84310 574 9
eISBN 978 1 84642 799 2

My Anxiety Handbook
Getting Back on Track
Sue Knowles, Bridie Gallagher and Phoebe McEwen
Illustrated by Emmeline Pidgen
ISBN 978 1 78592 440 8
eISBN 978 1 78450 813 5

THE ACT WORKBOOK FOR TEENS WITH OCD

UNHOOK YOURSELF AND
LIVE LIFE TO THE FULL

PATRICIA ZURITA ONA, PSY.D.

FOREWORD BY STUART RALPH

ILLUSTRATIONS BY LOUISE GARDNER

Jessica Kingsley *Publishers*
London and Philadelphia

First published in 2020
by Jessica Kingsley Publishers
73 Collier Street
London N1 9BE, UK
and
400 Market Street, Suite 400
Philadelphia, PA 19106, USA

www.jkp.com

Library of Congress Cataloging in Publication Data
A CIP catalog record for this book is available from the Library of Congress

British Library Cataloguing in Publication Data
A CIP catalogue record for this book is available from the British Library

ISBN 978 1 78775 083 8
eISBN 978 1 78775 084 5

Printed and bound in Great Britain

Contents

Foreword

When I think back to my teen years, there was definitely a lot I wasn't sure about and I felt confused and lost in this thing called OCD. It felt like I had a secret identity that I had to protect because of OCD, like a superhero. But unlike Superman, I wasn't born on the planet Krypton and I can't fly or run quicker than the eyes can see. Whereas Superman was protecting his superpowers, I was hiding my OCD for fear of being "mad," "crazy," or *insert any negative adjective here*. Some years later with therapy, time, and living by my values, I no longer hide. This new confidence has led me to create *The OCD Stories* podcast. It's a podcast in which I interview people with OCD, and some of the best OCD therapists around the world, all with the focus of providing teens, parents, and adults with resources to help them on their recovery journey—towards living the life they want. Through my podcast, I met the author of this book, Dr. Z.

From the moment we connected I could sense Dr. Z.'s passion, and knowledge for working with people with OCD. Dr. Z. owns and runs the East Bay Behavior Therapy Center in San Francisco where she works with teens affected by OCD, and helps them live life on their terms. She has an in-depth understanding of Exposure Response Prevention which is the gold standard of OCD treatment, and supercharges it with Acceptance and Commitment Therapy. Where these two worlds meet is the foundation of this book. Dr. Z. outlines what OCD is and the different treatments for it, and provides lots of exercises you can do within this book to unhook from your obsessions and start to see thoughts as just thoughts.

Dr. Z. uses a concept called the Choice Point to help you navigate situations when OCD is flaring up. Put simply, we always have a choice. A choice to move towards the things we value or away from them. It is at this

Choice Point that our life is shaped. That's easy to say, but in the grips of OCD it can definitely feel a million times harder than that. As a teen I never realized I had a choice, I always thought I had to do what OCD was telling me. Dr. Z.'s book aims to help you realize you always have a choice and that OCD can be worked through. Dr. Z. focuses in the latter part of this book on the life you want to create and live. This again connects with choice, the understanding that you can start to build the life you want to live based on the things you care about, and the meaningful goals you have.

Dr. Z. will talk about turning down your "fightonometer," about not fighting OCD, but instead making space for it. It is in the fight that we stir up OCD by trying to push it away, this process of pushing the thoughts away tells our brains these thoughts are important, so our brain gives them back to us. Whereas making space for those tricky thoughts and getting curious can help us work through them. Dr. Z. will give you some tools to turn down that "fightonometer" and see thoughts as thoughts. So, the fight is over. Put down the boxing gloves, and pick up your binoculars—it's time to get curious.

Recovery can be hard and messy at times, I don't know you personally, but I know you are a human and humans are pretty wonderful—especially teens—so I have faith you can work through this and create a life on your terms.

Stuart Ralph, *The OCD Stories*
London, UK

Letter to Teens

Dear Reader,

All the OCD workbooks I've read have very looooooooooong introductions, so I decided to keep it short and real. You're welcome!

Every day you wake up, so does your mind. And with it, the annoying, uninvited, and unsolicited obsessions wake up too. You're not alone! Many teenagers wrestle with those obsessions; they vary from being kind of bothersome to really disturbing, and they can boss you around, up and down, left to right, and back and forth.

These pesky obsessions come along with an automatic rush of fear and discomfort, and an unpleasant feeling that can push you to do all sorts of things that take you far away from the stuff that really matters to you.

I don't know how this book landed in your hands. Maybe your parents handed you this book or your therapist recommended that you read it, but I can tell you right away that no matter how these pages landed in your hands, this workbook is for *you*. These chapters have not been written by a researcher, manager of a program, or academic who studied OCD behind a desk and has never met an actual teenager, but by a therapist who has spent hours and hours working full time, with children, teens, and adults.

I know it would be nice to have a switch that you can just flick and make the obsessions go away so that you can relax, be stress-free, and have nothing to worry about, but sadly it doesn't work like that. Wherever you are, your mind is there with you, and the obsessions come along with it. But—and it's a big but—those pesky obsessions don't have to rule what you do with your life! In fact, the obsessions are not the problem; it's only when you put on your running shoes and avoid an obsession that you end up in Avoidance

City, or when you do compulsions that land in Compulsion City, or stop doing what's important and meaningful in your life, that things get rocky.

This workbook is a guide to help you to choose how to live your life day-by-day and to learn skills that will help you to hang in there with those dark obsessions so you can do what truly matters to you.

In the first section, you will learn the basics about OCD and research-based treatments, such as Exposure Response Prevention (ERP) and Acceptance and Commitment Therapy (ACT). Next, you will be introduced to the "Choice Point," a useful tool that will show you step-by-step how you get hooked on those obsessions and the costs of continuing to do the same thing over and over in your life. After learning about the price of living in safety country, as I call it, you will be invited to step back and check in with yourself about what you actually care about. In the rest of the book you will learn powerful skills to unhook from your obsessions, including values-guided exposure exercises, so that you can move forward with the stuff that is important to you.

As a bonus, I have created a website where you can access additional activities and exercises: www.actbeyondocd.com. Check it out!

When you're done with this workbook, you will be ready to find your Choice Point every time an obsession pops up and you will have the skills to choose how to respond to it. Will you move towards or away from what matters to you? There is no one better than *you* to choose.

So let's get you going with your life!

Warmly,
Dr. Z.

Letter for Parents

Dear Parent or Caregiver,

How many times have you thought, "It's exhausting dealing with OCD" and wondered, "How did this happen?" How many times have you felt like screaming because your teen is asking you to do something for him over and over? How many times have you struggled because of an OCD episode at home? How many times has your mind told you, "It's my fault?"

If your teen is dealing with OCD, or you suspect that's the case, I know that it's not easy for you and it's not easy for your teen. It's not your fault and it's not your teen's fault either. This workbook will help your teen to learn how to handle those pesky obsessions and move forward in life!

As your teen will learn in this workbook, at some point, everyone has uncomfortable and unwanted thoughts. However, what feeds an OCD episode is when your teen takes those intrusive thoughts very seriously and manages their fear with compulsions and avoidant behaviors, which may involve asking you and others to make all types of accommodations to calm down their anxiety.

The chapters in this book are focused on specific research-based skills: Acceptance and Commitment Therapy (ACT) and Exposure Response Prevention (ERP). These skills will help your teen to catch those obsessions, hang in there with the fear that comes with them, and choose how to continue moving forward with what matters in their day-to-day life.

If you have a chance, take a peek at this workbook to get familiar with the skills your teen will learn chapter by chapter. I also have a website where you and your teen can access extra information on OCD, ACT, and ERP, as well as additional exercises and activities: www.actbeyondocd.com.

This workbook is about encouraging your teen to choose when to face his fears, how to do it, and, ultimately, how to handle fear, anxiety, and discomfort as part of life. And as I encourage your teen to choose, I encourage you to do the same. Parenting is really hard, challenging, and exhausting at times, but instead of pushing through or powering through it, I invite you to step back, hold on to your parenting values and choose how to support your teen when things are difficult.

Warmly,
Dr. Z.

Letter for Therapists

Dear Colleague,

I'm excited to introduce you to this workbook to augment the clinical work you're already doing with teens struggling with OCD. If you're a newbie to ACT, or a newbie to treating OCD, you now have the perfect workbook to guide you through every session, add Acceptance and Commitment Therapy (ACT) and Exposure Response Prevention (ERP) to your skills repertoire, and reduce the challenges you may experience when helping a client with unwanted obsessions.

Here is what's unique about this workbook:

1. It's not written from the desk of an academic or a researcher but from a therapist's office. I do what you do, full time, hour by hour.

2. It's the outcome of years of thinking about how to make ERP accessible to teens dealing with obsessions. They don't like to be told what to do, but they like to know they can choose.

3. It teaches teens that fears, anxiety, worry, and nervousness are part of life: they feel them, they think them, and they just happen. Teens learn chapter by chapter how to make room to hang out with them, instead of being held back by them.

4. It brings ACT down-to-earth and brings to the forefront the Choice Point—a tool to help teens to exercise a core skill: their capacity to choose how to face their fears when it matters to them to do so.

5. It teaches teens new skills to handle the stream of pesky obsessions that show up in their mind—not as enemies to fight against—but as ongoing chains of letters, words, or images put together that can be watched, sung, teased, jotted down, and even played with.

6. It's the result of my drive to disseminate treatments that work and can make a difference in a teen's life.

You can use this workbook as a roadmap for your clinical work because it will walk you and the teens you work with through different skills they can apply right away to move forward in life while carrying along the obsessions that pop up here and there in their mind. You will have a chance to have conversations that matter with your clients!

The workbook teaches your clients how to use the Choice Point, gives them tons of skills to practice, and provides exercises to identify what really matters to them. It supports them to make a shift from engaging in compulsions and avoidant behaviors and introduces values-guided exposures as a way of helping them to choose to feel with openness, curiosity, and flexibility!

After getting familiar with this workbook, you can dip in and out and use sections with clients as needed—play with these tools and dance with them in your clinical work! Remember, therapy is never a linear process but a curvy one. And, if you want extra materials, be sure to check out my website: www.actbeyondocd.com.

I was introduced to ACT approximately 15 years ago, and to the Choice Point, co-created by Joseph Ciarrochi, Ann Bailey, and Russ Harris, five years ago.[1] Over the years of working with people with OCD, anxiety, and related conditions, there was something I quickly noticed: there is no winning with our mind, and every time we argue, fight back, or try to convince it of something else, we're just losing time that we could be spending doing the stuff that we care about. I have written down, used, drawn, and even acted out the Choice Point to talk about ACT, map how OCD episodes happen, organize my exposure sessions, and foster my client's capacity to choose to get out of safety country when it matters to them. And I can tell you that the teens love it and I absolutely love it too!

---

1   Ciarrochi, J., Bailey, A., and Harris, R. (2014) *The Weight Escape: How to Stop Dieting and Start Living*. Boston, MA: Shambhala Publications.

I personally think that OCD is a unique language-based struggle because clients get quickly hooked by their obsessions and are so trapped by the thought "I need to do something right here, right now" that they end up spending too much time in their heads rather than living life. ACT behavioral interventions—like the ones you will learn in this workbook—are extremely powerful and impactful in getting our clients unhooked and taking steps with their mouth, feet, and hands towards the stuff that truly matters to them.

And, as with many things in life, reading and talking about it is not the same as doing it. So, practice and practice putting ACT and the Choice Point into action in your work with OCD!

Warmly,

Dr. Z.

Tips for Using This Workbook

If you are reading this workbook it is because you're interested in learning how to handle Obsessive Compulsive Disorder (OCD) and live your life to the full. Even though I don't know you, I know you're doing your best, and I value the choice you're making by trying out this workbook. So, I want to give you some recommendations to help you make the best use of all the skills covered in this workbook:

MAKE THIS WORKBOOK YOURS!

This workbook has been written for YOU! If there are any exercises, activities, or tips you like and find helpful, by all means feel free to circle, underline, highlight, note down, or make any mark you want to recognize them in some way.

When identifying your values or the stuff you care about, make sure to make a special mark since you will need to go back to those pages over and over.

There is no wrong way of doing anything in this workbook. Your choice to do things is more important than anything else!

COMPLETE ALL THE ACTIVITIES AND EXERCISES IN EVERY CHAPTER

All the chapters in this workbook have exercises to help you to learn, try, and remember a skill from Acceptance and Commitment Therapy (ACT), help you to figure out how to live with annoying worries, anxieties, and obsessions, and how to create the amazing life you want to live.

When working on this workbook, keep in mind that there is a difference between reading about an exercise versus trying it; it's only when you try and participate in these exercises that you will have a sense of what works for you and what doesn't. So don't skip any of the activities from this workbook!

SET ASIDE TIME TO READ THIS WORKBOOK

I would recommend you schedule in at least 10 minutes for each chapter. Most of the chapters are short and, generally, 10–15 minutes will allow you to zoom into each chapter, complete the exercises, and see how you can apply the skill into your daily life.

EXPECT SOME REPETITION OF CORE IDEAS OR THEMES

Some ideas and themes will come up again and again in the workbook. This repetition is not to bore you, but because these ideas are core concepts that will give you a frame of reference when putting all the other skills into action.

PACE YOUR READING

Working on this project is not a school project, but I suggest that you read at a rate of one or two chapters per week and no more than that. All of the chapters are short and easy to read, but there is no need to rush through the material all at once. Learning new skills takes time.

For Sections 6 and 7, "Getting Unhooked!" and "Specialized Unhooking Skills," I would encourage you to focus on just one chapter a week because those sections include core skills to practice. Trying these core skills only once is not enough; ideally, you will practice them multiple times over a week (at least!) to become familiar with them and really see how they work for you.

BE PATIENT WHEN LEARNING AND PRACTICING NEW SKILLS

With the exception of the informative chapters in Section 1, all of the chapters introduce you to a new skill. Some of these skills may be familiar to you, but others may not, and some of them may even seem silly. But if at any point you find yourself getting frustrated with your progress, I invite you to be patient with yourself—it takes time to learn any new skill and it takes time to bring it into your life.

PRACTICE BEING PRESENT IN THE MOMENT

Being present in the moment—being mindful or being aware is an important skill within ACT. You don't need to have your eyes closed all the time to practice mindfulness. You can practice awareness on-the-go, at school, home, the movie theater, or anywhere else you happen to be! Being aware is all about being focused on what's happening in the moment, *so you just need to be present* to practice mindfulness. In this workbook you will have a chance to practice many activities that have awareness exercises built in already. However, I encourage you to check out the website www. actbeyondocd.com to practice extra awareness exercises, so you can get better and better at handling those pesky obsessions and doing what you care about.

OPTIONAL: USE THIS WORKBOOK AS PART OF THERAPY

This workbook has been written as a stand-alone workbook for any teen struggling with Obsessive Compulsive Disorder. However, you might also find it helpful if you're currently working with a therapist. A therapist familiar with Acceptance and Commitment Therapy (ACT) will understand right away the approach in this workbook.

THE BEGINNING

You might expect an introduction to a section of a workbook to tell you what the section is about and what to expect when reading it, right? I'll certainly do that, I promise. But first I want to briefly tell you the story behind this workbook. I promise this is not going to be a lecture!

Years ago, I worked with Amy, a 12-year-old struggling with "fears of not being honest enough," and who got triggered when taking tests and when talking to her parents. She tried really hard to make sure she didn't cheat at school, asked her classmates not to let her see their work, asked her parents if they saw her doing anything that wasn't truthful, and told her parents everything that happened during a day, even when they didn't ask about it. Amy received treatment for these fears for three to four months with a therapist close to her home, and then with another one near her school, but after all of that, she ended up having a screaming match with her parents and refused to go back to see anyone. Time passed by and Amy and her parents decided to try "that therapy thing" one more time, and that's how they ended up in my office. Amy shared something with me that became the key idea behind the workbook you're holding in your hands right now. Amy was told all the time by her parents and therapists that she needed to overcome OCD. Amy knew it was important, but she hated feeling forced and not having a voice in how and when to face the things she found scary.

This was the beginning of my personal quest to figure out how to make treatments for OCD more impactful and suitable for my teen clients so they don't give up on treatment and let their obsessions boss them around throughout their lives. After years of learning about Acceptance and Commitment Therapy (ACT), I tried many skills over and over in my work with adults, teens, and kids, and even though things were going well, there was still something missing. And that's when I realized that the Choice Point was the missing piece of this puzzle.

The Choice Point works with our natural capacity to decide, pick, and choose how to interact with the world around us—including objects, people, situations, and all the other types of things that surround us—and how to handle all the stuff that happens under our skin, like thoughts, feelings, doubts, worries, impulses, and so many other hundreds of things.

The Choice Point was exactly what my teen clients needed, and what you need when facing scary obsessions in your life, because, in those moments of discomfort, anxiety, and panic, as hard as it sounds, you forget that you can *choose* and that there's no one better than *you* to make that choice!

This first section is the beginning of a new and amazing journey you are about to take with this workbook. It's the starting point for you to choose how to respond to your obsessions, how to live your life, and how to continue moving along with the things that matter to you even when fearful situations arise in your day-to-day life.

Choosing to face a fearful situation can be scary in the beginning, but it's also essential if we want to shape our life the way we want it. It's like a coin with two sides. On one side there is a life we want to live, and on the other side, the fear, struggles, doubts, and other unpleasant experiences that come along with it. There is no other way—you can't have one side without the other!

Let's get you started on this new beginning!

CHAPTER 1

The Basics about OCD

Do you ever find yourself hanging out with your friends and then an image of pushing one of them pops into your mind? Do you ever feel scared of getting sick because you touched a credit card? Do you have moments when suddenly you have a hard-to-let-go feeling about something being wrong if you don't re-write sentences on your homework? Do you stop yourself from walking over a crack on the sidewalk because of a sudden sensation that doing so feels wrong? Do you sometimes spend hours replaying a situation to make sure you didn't do anything morally inappropriate? Do you text your friends multiple times a day to make sure they're not upset with you? Do you email your teacher just to make sure you didn't cheat in the test?

If you answered yes to any of those questions, even one of them, chances are you might be dealing with Obsessive Compulsive Disorder (OCD). However, the above sentences are just some examples of the experiences of people with OCD. You may identify with them or you might have different obsessions. Either way, if you have OCD, what's happening is that your brain is working really hard to feed you with fear, doubt, anxiety, distress, and panic at all times, and sometimes more than others.

There are key elements that together make OCD a problem in your life. Let's briefly go over each one of them so you can get familiar with them:

1. *Obsessions* are all the unwanted, intrusive, and uninvited thoughts, images, sensations, or impulses that pop into your mind over and over and are scary, annoying, distressing, and totally irritating.

2. *Compulsions* are everything you do to try to minimize, neutralize, push away, and get rid of your obsessions and turn down the fear, anxiety, and distress that come along with the obsessions.

3. *Avoidance* or escape refers to all the behaviors you do to run away from a fearful situation as if you're wearing your fastest running shoes so that you end up not having to face the scary situation.

4. *Short-term consequences*: Are all the consequences that happen right away because of compulsions, avoidance, and escaping behaviors that seem to work in the short term because they can make your fear, anxiety, and distress go away really quickly.

But compulsions and avoidance have...

5. *long-term consequences in your day-to-day life*: The combination of getting too scared about an obsession and responding to that fear with avoidance and compulsions is what makes up an OCD episode. When this cycle repeats itself over and over, you end up with a bunch of OCD episodes to the point that you stop doing the stuff you care about. Your life gets smaller and smaller, narrower and narrower, and managing OCD becomes an unpaid full-time job for you!

Take a look at the OCD map that follows which illustrates how OCD episodes occur, one after another, and how all the key elements interact together, over and over!

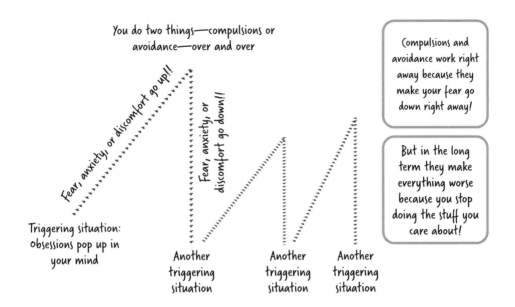

You do two things—compulsions or avoidance—over and over

Fear, anxiety, or discomfort go up!!

Fear, anxiety, or discomfort go down!!

Triggering situation: obsessions pop up in your mind

Another triggering situation

Another triggering situation

Another triggering situation

Compulsions and avoidance work right away because they make your fear go down right away!

But in the long term they make everything worse because you stop doing the stuff you care about!

Let's consider Louis' story. Louis is patting his cat, Oliver, and while doing so, he has a disturbing image in his mind of stabbing Oliver that shows up out of the blue and is hard to let go, dismiss, or ignore. That's an *obsession*. He gets very scared because he loves Oliver, and, although he knows he wouldn't ever stab his cat, he drops Oliver, starts crying, tells his dad that he could do bad things to Oliver, and that he doesn't know if the cat is going to be safe with him. For the next three weeks, Louis manages this obsession by doing two things: (1) he avoids holding Oliver and refuses to be in a room alone with his cat; and (2) he also asks his dad and mom multiple times if Oliver is safe or if they have seen him doing anything bad to Oliver. Those are *compulsions*. Every time Louis avoids being with Oliver or engages in a compulsion, he quickly feels better, and is relieved at the idea that he did not hurt his cat. Those are the *short-term consequences*. Then suddenly, a couple days later, Louis has another image in which he punches his parents. He gets even more scared, does other compulsions, and avoids situations that involve being with his parents. He also stops playing with Oliver and stops hanging out with his friends to avoid doing something hurtful to them. In three months, the *long-term consequences* are that Louis has ended up feeling sad, really sad, because he doesn't know what's going on. He continues to have these annoying obsessions, and continues with compulsions and avoidant behaviors one after another. Here is a graphic that shows Louis' OCD episodes:

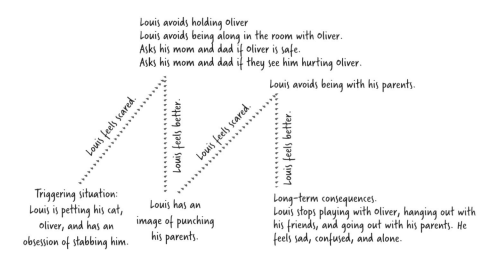

What Louis doesn't know is that almost everyone experiences unwanted thoughts, images, and urges at some point in life, including aggressive and weird ones. Louis doesn't know that doing compulsions and avoidant behaviors keeps OCD running until living with OCD becomes a full-time job and that OCD can cause him to miss out on the fun, creative, athletic, or academic activities that he enjoys, stopping him from living his life to the full.

In the next section, "The Choice Point Meets OCD," you will have a chance to map how you go through an OCD episode in your day-to-day life and what happens to your life when that occurs. For now, I just want to give you a brief review of the basics and a share a big message with you: As annoying as your obsessions are, they're not the problem—it is relying on avoidance and compulsive behaviors that makes things worse for you. Little by little, you will learn different skills to handle those unwelcome obsessions without shrinking your life and to take steps towards the stuff that matters to you!

I don't know how familiar you were with OCD before you started reading this book but, now that you have learnt something about the key elements of OCD, you may wonder…

ARE THERE DIFFERENT TYPES OF OCD?

Most academics, researchers, and clinicians agree and have written about the sub-types of OCD, including:

◎ contamination

- aggression

- symmetry

- sexual orientation

- scrupulosity

- relationships

- religious

- responsibility

- existential

- meta-physical.

Any obsession that doesn't fit within those categories is usually called a miscellaneous obsession.

Here is an important clarification for you: Although the literature speaks about sub-types of OCD and it may look like there are different types of OCD, these sub-types only exist because they refer to the theme of obsessions. Whatever sub-type you're dealing with, or a combination of them, or maybe you start with a theme of an obsession and then it shifts into another one, they all respond to the same treatment principles and no type is worse than the other.

And to make it crystal clear, all forms of obsessions share a common factor: they come along with tons of fear, anxiety, and distress that push you to take them seriously, as absolute truths, and without even checking that they make sense, just like Louis who feared he would hurt the cat he loves.

All of the skills you will learn in this workbook apply to any sub-type of obsession you may be dealing with. You won't need to do any extra reading about any particular sub-type. Right now, the most important thing for you is to learn and apply skills to deal with OCD and move forward with your life!

IT'S YOUR CHOICE

It's quite likely that your parents or friends, or perhaps even a therapist, have said to you at some point, "Just stop, don't worry about it," as if it were that easy to stop the cycle of OCD. Maybe your parents and caregivers sometimes acted as the OCD police, and while that advice may have sometimes been helpful, I promise you that you won't hear those words or that type of advice in this workbook. This workbook isn't about pushing or forcing you to do something you don't want to do, it's actually the opposite: this workbook is about teaching you ACT skills to handle those ultra-annoying obsessions and compulsions, figure out what's truly important to you, face fearful situations when you are ready to do so, and move forward with your life! This workbook is about letting you choose all the way!

In each chapter you will find different forms, word games to complete, and places to draw, so you don't get bored when reading this workbook! And of course, each of these activities aims to help you to learn, remember, and practice specific skills to manage uninvited obsessions, and put into action life skills to handle any scary situation that your mind comes up with today, tomorrow, and for the rest of your life!

No one can choose for you how you respond to those irritating obsessions, and no one better than *you* can *choose* how to live your life!

ACTIVITY

How about completing the crossword below based on what you learned in this chapter? Go for it!

CLUES

Down

1. An obsession is an _____ thought, image, or urge.

2. A common and strong emotion that comes along with obsessions.

3. _____ get rid of an obsession right away.

Across

4. Compulsions work in the _____ _____.

5. _____ are a form of obsession.

6. A sub-type of OCD.

You will find the answers at the end of the book in Appendix 7.

CHAPTER 2

The Basics of Treatment and This Workbook

Whether you have been recently diagnosed with OCD, you suspect you're dealing with OCD, or your parents have told you that they think you have OCD, you may have questions about treatment and whether this workbook is going to be helpful to you. In this chapter, you will read about treatment options and get a good sense of where this workbook is coming from.

I'll start by going over two treatments for OCD: Exposure Response Prevention (ERP) and Acceptance and Commitment Therapy (ACT). Don't worry, you won't be reading a boring academic article, you will read just enough information to understand what treatment looks like and how this workbook can be super-helpful for you in tackling OCD episodes and learning to keep doing or do more of the stuff you care about. Let's zoom into it!

WHAT IS ERP?

You may wonder, what the heck is Exposure Response Prevention (ERP)? To start with, ERP is the most effective, research-based treatment for OCD and anxiety-related conditions. In a nutshell, ERP is about learning how to handle the unwanted obsessions you're scared of and the feelings of fear, discomfort, and panic that come along with them.

Do you remember Louis from the previous chapter? He had an aggressive obsession about stabbing his cat Oliver, even though he was an animal lover, adored his cat, and wouldn't ever hurt him. When Louis participated in ERP treatment, some of his ERP exercises included activities like sitting close to his cat Oliver while having the thought "What if I stab him?" or holding Oliver in his arms while holding also a knife.

And just to clarify, ERP is not about torturing Louis. It is about exposing him to the thoughts, images, or ideas that scare him, helping him to face this very scary obsession so he can get back to playing with Oliver and move forward with the stuff that he really cares about.

ERP is the frontline treatment for OCD and related conditions, and this workbook is not only based on ERP, but also on ACT. Which leads to the question...

WHAT IS ACT?

ACT, pronounced as one single word ("act"), stands for Acceptance and Commitment Therapy. It is a very well-researched treatment that approaches ERP and exposure-based interventions with a unique spin.

ACT starts by helping you figure out the stuff you care about as a starting point before doing anything or facing any scary situation. For example, ACT helped Louis to identify his personal value of "being caring with animals." From there, you learn ACT skills to handle all those bizarre obsessions that pop up in your mind, choose when and how to face those fearful situations that take away from what you care about, and take specific actions to expand your life all the way! Every skill in this workbook, and everything you do within ACT, is with the intention of helping you do the things you care about and live life to the full. For Louis, ACT helped him to go back to playing with Oliver, hanging out with his parents, and spending time with his classmates from school.

And just to clarify, exposure is a skill already embedded within ACT, because doing what matters to you is not easy-peasy all the time, and it's quite likely that every time you're doing the stuff you care about, there are going to be all types of mind noise, challenging feelings, and annoying unwanted thoughts, images, and urges coming along. In this workbook, you will learn ACT and ERP skills together step-by-step, so you can get the best of both treatments to reclaim your life from OCD episodes. And to practice all the ACT and ERP skills you're going to be introduced to a really cool tool: the Choice Point.

WHAT IS THE CHOICE POINT?

Let me give you some brief background info about this useful tool.

In 2013, three ACT psychologists, Joseph Ciarrochi, Ann Bailey, and Russ Harris, spent hours thinking how about how to make ACT approachable for clients struggling with weight issues, so they co-created the Choice Point. A couple of years later, in 2015, one of them, Russ Harris, decided to tweak it to make it more accessible to people with all types of struggles, not just problems related to weight. Years later, Dr. Z. (that's me!) went on a mission searching for different ways to make ACT and exposure work more impactful, less stuffy, less wordy, and easy to grasp. So, after testing it out with her students and clients, she made a slight adjustment to the Choice Point to make it applicable to the treatment of OCD.

The Choice Point will help you to keep track of what you're doing every time those obsessions show up in your mind, and to check whether your actions help you get closer or further away from the stuff that matters to you, the things you really care about. But, to be honest, I think one of my favorite reasons to introduce you to the Choice Point is that it will help you to remember a skill you already have but may have forgotten to use: your ability to choose how to live your life, how to handle those defiant OCD episodes, and how to deal with all types of fearful and uncomfortable situations that will come along in your life sooner or later. Whether you are 11, 15, or 17 years old, and even when you reach your thirties, forties, fifties, and beyond, you will encounter scary moments in your life, as I do, and as everyone does. They are part of life.

Little by little, as impossible as it sounds, with this workbook you will remember how to put into action your ability to choose in so many ways: choosing how to live your life, how to be the person you want to be, how to face what you're scared of, how to take steps towards what you care about, or how to choose what you care about!

And when you're done with this workbook, you will put the Choice Point into action in your everyday life regardless of where you are, who you're with, or what mind noise your mind comes up with!

ACTIVITY

For this chapter's activity, see if you can find the hidden key words and acronyms in this word search puzzle: (1) choice, (2) exposure, (3) ERP, and (4) ACT.

Z	O	S	U	F	S	O	G	N	P	U
A	Y	E	M	F	R	J	I	R	B	Y
N	B	C	H	O	I	C	E	H	W	G
A	J	B	E	J	W	R	D	E	Z	B
B	U	S	Q	R	N	Q	S	D	E	O
B	Q	E	V	B	U	M	O	O	B	O
P	E	K	Z	Q	A	S	U	H	V	W
V	F	V	Q	B	O	W	O	I	H	R
A	H	Y	U	S	T	R	W	P	X	E
N	T	C	A	H	N	R	Q	R	X	R
U	B	I	Y	I	Q	B	M	K	A	E

CHAPTER 3

Why Do I Have to Deal with OCD?

At some point in the ACT/ERP treatment process, the teens I work with sooner or later usually ask me questions along the lines of: Dr. Z., why do I have to deal with OCD? Why did it have to be me who ended up having OCD?

You may find yourself with similar questions, so I will do my best to answer them with a short and science-based response: if you're dealing with OCD or anxiety-related problems, chances are the danger detector of your brain—the amygdala—is working ultra-hard, sending you many fearful and panicky signals about those obsessions showing up in your mind. It's like your brain automatically assumes that every uncomfortable and distressing thought, image, or impulse you have is dangerous, just like that, and without even considering other variables. Interesting, right?

You may be curious—why is my brain working super-hard in this way?

There are three possibilities for you to consider when answering that question: (1) having brain chemistry imbalances and genetic predisposition; (2) observing others; and (3) having OCD-related associations. Let's consider them one-by-one, so you can check which ones apply to you.

HAVING BRAIN CHEMISTRY IMBALANCES AND GENETIC PREDISPOSITION TO ANXIETY

I don't mean to give you a lecture in brain functioning, but just want you to be aware that there are different-held views of brain chemistry imbalances and genetics when looking at the causes of OCD: (1) there is a long-held view that OCD is caused by deficiencies in serotonin and dopamine, which are chemical messengers in the brain; (2) a second view posits that OCD is genetically transmitted; and (3) a final view suggests that a person suffering with OCD has a different brain structure. However, despite the popularity of all these explanations, scientists and researchers have not fully supported any of them up to this point (Jenike *et al.* 1991;[1] Goldstein *et al.* 1994),[2] but at least now you're familiar with them.

Some families are more "predisposed" to having anxiety, but that doesn't necessarily mean that if your grandmother was anxious, you will develop OCD. It just means that in some families there is genetic susceptibility to develop anxiety.

WATCHING OTHERS STRUGGLING WITH OCD

It's conceivable that you started showing OCD behaviors after observing others in your household or school displaying some compulsions or avoidance behaviors. While this is possible, this hypothesis does not explain the extent to which some people struggle with OCD while others are able to manage their obsessions, suggesting that observing or living with others struggling with OCD may not be the sole cause of it.

MAKING CONNECTIONS BETWEEN AN OBSESSION AND FEAR-BASED RESPONSES

It's also possible that in a given moment, any moment, your brain came up with an awful intrusive image that came along with tons of fear, dread, and panic. And of course, your brain, as it usually does with everything, quickly and forever made a connection between that "unwanted obsession" and fear-based reactions. For example, Samantha was watching a movie with her youngest brother and, out of the blue, she had an image of stabbing him—that's an unwanted obsession. Samantha got very, very scared and took that

---

1   Jenike, M.A., Baer, H.T., Ballantine, R.L., Martuza, S. *et al.* (1991) 'Cingulotomy for refractory obsessive-compulsive disorder: A long-term follow-up of 33 patients.' *Archives of General Psychiatry 48*, 6, 548–555.

2   Goldstein, R.B., Weissman, M.M., Adams, P.B., Horwath, E. *et al.* (1994) 'Psychiatric disorders in relatives or probands with panic disorder and/or major depression.' *Archives of General Psychiatry 51*, 5, 383–394.

image as an absolute truth, and then, really quickly, she started avoiding being around her brother and hanging out alone with him because her brain made a connection between fear and anything related to her brother.

Even though these potential causes may have limitations in fully explaining how you ended up with OCD if taken individually, it's helpful to consider them, because they show that it is not your fault that you are dealing with OCD, that dealing with OCD doesn't mean that something is wrong with you, and that dealing with OCD is only a sign that your brain is working super-duper, ultra-hard, and seeing every obsession as dangerous right away. You're not broken, just wired to think a lot!

Whatever the cause of your OCD, the ACT and ERP skills apply to you, regardless of how your OCD started and/or the type of OCD you're dealing with.

As an ACT therapist with passion for behavior therapy, I would like to remind you that, as you learned in the introduction to Section 1, what keeps OCD episodes happening has nothing to do with those annoying obsessions showing up in your mind. Although it's an uncomfortable experience, having an unwanted thought doesn't lead to OCD and most of us have totally bizarre thoughts in our life at one point or another.

OCD episodes occur because when those pesky obsessions show up, you get hooked on them, take them and the feelings that come along with it very seriously, forget that you can choose how to handle them, and end up doing compulsions and avoidant behaviors over and over. This reinforces the association between the obsession and fear-based responses, feeds the OCD cycle, and creates a full-time job for you.

Moving forward, you will learn new ways to handle those obsessions and practice your natural choosing skills.

ACTIVITY

For this activity, take a look at the table below and, based on what you know about yourself and your family, answer each question.

Possible causes of OCD	Write your response here....
Does someone in your family experience anxiety?	
Have you observed others struggling with OCD either at home, school, or even on social media?	
Do you recall the first time in which your brain connected an obsession with intense fear?	
Other possibilities you can come up with…	

CHAPTER 4

Why Do I Have to Deal with Fear?

After reading about different causes of OCD, you may still wonder why you have to deal with fear when it's such an unpleasant emotion. Here is my honest and science-based response: Whether you're in Bolivia, London, California, Sydney, China, Iran, or anywhere in the world, regardless of your age, ethnicity, sexual orientation, or gender identification, you're wired to experience fear and anxiety and all the variations of those emotions, such as worry, panic, stress, nervousness, or dread. Going through those uncomfortable emotions is unavoidable, because as much as you and I don't like them, those emotions are part of being alive—and no doctor can perform a surgery to remove your capacity to feel those unpleasant emotions!

Even though we're biologically equipped to have those distressing emotions, you may have received tons of negative messages about them, and have been encouraged to do all types of things to make sure you never feel them. Let's take a look at what you have learned about fear and anxiety!

To start, write down all the messages you have heard or learned about fear, anxiety, panic, and related emotions up to this point. Louis, from Chapter 1, wrote:

I was told that I shouldn't be afraid ever.

Your turn!

_____

_____

_____

_____

_____

_____

_____

_____

Any reactions when writing down those messages? Were they positive or negative? Have you ever heard that you shouldn't feel afraid of anything or that you just have to power through things when feeling scared?

Most of us have received messages about fear-related responses not being good emotions and about how controlling or getting rid of them is the only way to manage them. But the truth is that we'll continue to experience fearful moments in our day-to-day life regardless of any attempts to control or banish them, just because we're alive.

Are you open to recalling fearful memories you may have had the last year? Can you draw three of those fearful moments? If you prefer, you can write down your responses.

Fearful memory 1	Fearful memory 2	Fearful memory 3

Now jot down what you did to handle the fear that came with each of those memories. For example: Louis recalled feeling very scared when looking down from a very high bridge in London. He handled his fear by closing his eyes whenever he was crossing that bridge. Your turn.

FEARFUL MEMORY 1

_____

_____

FEARFUL MEMORY 2

_____

_____

FEARFUL MEMORY 3

_____

_____

How was it for you to recall those memories? We really do everything we can to handle fear, but sometimes we forget to notice that fear can also drive very helpful behavior. For example, Louis remembered that one day, when he was walking down the street, he looked to the left and saw a car driving really fast. He got scared about potentially being hit by it, so stopped walking, and waited for the car to go past him.

What about you? Can you recall three memories in which fear, anxiety, and panic may have been helpful to you?

MEMORY OF FEAR BEING HELPFUL 1

_____

_____

MEMORY OF FEAR BEING HELPFUL 2

_____

_____

MEMORY OF FEAR BEING HELPFUL 3

_____

_____

How was it for you to remember moments in which fear and other related emotions may have been helpful? Sometimes my clients say "Dr. Z., why do I have to remember something that was bad and scary? I don't like it." Many people will tell you to forget those memories, and instead focus on positive, happy, and cheerful ones. However, we don't have the power to make fear, anxiety, and all types of uncomfortable emotions go away completely. The local shop doesn't sell a device that removes fear from our natural disposition as human beings!

We all try to get rid of scared feelings sometimes, but here is the catch: the harder we try to push down fear, worry, anxiety, or any variation of those feelings, the more we have them. Even if you use distractions such as listening to music, skateboarding, or watching movies when feeling scared, and the fear goes down a bit, it's a matter of time before it shows up again and again, in your day-to-day life.

Fear, anxiety, nervousness, uneasiness, apprehension, or dread are like any other feelings we experience, such as joy, excitement, and happiness— we can't control them. However, we can control what to do with our feet, hands, and mouth when fear and its buddies show up, so we can focus on living with them and living well. What about moving forward and choosing how to respond to those overwhelming feelings in a way that is consistent with who you want to be?

TAKEAWAYS!

Congratulations, you're done with Section 1! In this section you got the basics of what OCD is, how your brain works, how doing compulsions and avoiding things that are important to you maintains OCD and shrinks your life, and how ACT can help you to have great relationships, fun, and joy as you move forward.

You don't have to be defined by OCD. With practice, patience, and dedication, you can learn to break from OCD symptoms and live an amazing life! You got this!

THE CHOICE POINT MEETS OCD

Imagine for a second that you read in the news that "Iron Man and Thor meet to watch the new Superman movie." How would that be? Can you imagine that? It might be interesting, strange, and maybe even fun. But it may make no sense to you—why would Iron Man and Thor hang out to watch a Superman movie?

Now, here is a title that does make total sense: The Choice Point meets OCD. And the following is why this title makes sense.

As much as we don't like them, obsessions happen, anxiety happens, and fear happens. We don't have control of what shows up under our skin—our mind and emotions do their own thing and their own thinking! Emotions can get turned on and off, anytime, anywhere. And sometimes the more we don't want to have an annoying experience, the more we have it. But, while all this activity is constantly happening inside us, we do have the capacity to choose how to respond to those fears and obsessions.

In this section, the Choice Point will remind you exactly what you can forget when feeling triggered with unsolicited obsessions: to *choose* how to respond to them! You can choose how to behave even when all types of background noise is going on in your mind and body. And moving forward, this workbook will show you exactly that: how to find your own Choice Point when your mind—like a Chihuahua—barks and barks all types of obsessions!

As impossible and as hard as it sounds, you actually have many moments of choice throughout your day, one after another, one minute after another minute, and basically, with every obsession that pops up, there is your Choice Point. Do you go along with the obsession or do you choose to do what you care about?

You can choose, over and over!

CHAPTER 5

Getting to Know Your OCD

In Chapter 1, you briefly learned about the different components of the OCD package. In this chapter, you're going to zoom into each one of those components and check how they show up in your day-to-day activities so you can get better and better at catching OCD before it catches you. Let's do this!

KNOW THIS!

Do you remember the OCD map from Chapter 1? Here it is again, and this time we're going to break it down, part-by-part and piece-by-piece, with a bit more detail than the first time.

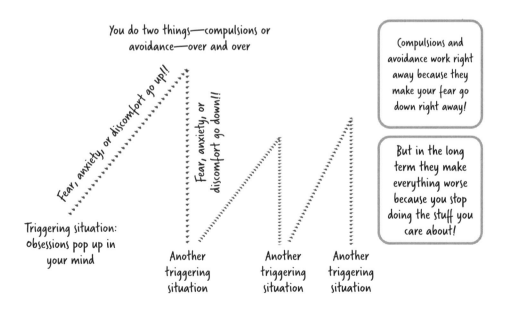

Let's go over one more time the components you need to know about from the above OCD map:

1. *Triggering situations* are all things that start an OCD episode. They can be external, such as an object, place, person, or even a sound or smell; or internal, such as a memory, a physical sensation, or a feeling, to name a few.

   Let's go over an example: Norah, a 14-year-old, was scared about cursing bad words about Latino people. This was her obsession. Her OCD episodes got triggered every time she saw a Latino classmate or went to a Latino restaurant. These were her external triggers. When Norah remembered the trip she took to Spain with her family, she also got triggered and wasn't sure whether she cursed at someone or not. These memories were her internal triggers.

2. *Obsessions*, as you know by now, are all the unwanted, nonsensical, and uncontrollable thoughts, images, or impulses that show up unexpectedly in your mind, out of the blue, and that keep showing up and are just hard to have.

   For Norah, the obsession that popped up over and over in her mind was her fear about cursing a Latino person.

3. *Compulsions* are all the things you do to stop those annoying obsessions from happening or from proving they're true.

   Norah, for example, blinks her eyes twice as quickly as possible and presses her thumb against her index fingers a couple of times to make sure she doesn't scream obscenities to her Latino friends. Those behaviors are called compulsions because she's doing them with the purpose of preventing her from cursing and reducing the anxiety, fear, and discomfort that comes along with that obsession.

4. *Escaping or avoidant behaviors*, as you may recall, refer to all behaviors you do to avoid facing a trigger for fear that it may start an OCD episode.

   Norah didn't attend her friends' gathering just to avoid seeing her Latino classmates and getting triggered; she also avoided Latino markets when going grocery shopping with her mom. Every time that

Norah doesn't show up to the stuff that matters to her, it's called an escaping or avoidant response.

5. *Short-term consequences* are what happen right after engaging in compulsions and escaping or avoidant behaviors.

In Norah's case, as soon as she blinks her eyes quickly or tells her mom she cannot go into a particular Latino store, her fear, anxiety, and discomfort go down quickly. For her, as for you, and for everyone dealing with OCD and anxiety, a short-term consequence of these behaviors is feeling better right away, and that's why people keep engaging in these responses hundreds of times. Tricky, right?

6. *The long-term consequences* in your life are the price you pay every time you engage in compulsions, avoidance, and escaping behaviors. And this is exactly where OCD really has a larger impact because, instead of spending all your time and energy doing fun stuff—hanging out with your friends, enjoying your family's company, dreaming about what you want your life to be about, and discovering new hobbies and passions—those compulsions and avoidant behaviors take you further and further away from where you really want to go. It's like you want to go north and all those strategies to minimize, get rid of, and suppress obsessions take you south.

For Norah, the long-term consequence of getting hooked on obsessions and doing compulsions and avoidant behaviors is that she feels frustrated with herself for not doing the things she cares about, sad because she's not spending as much time as she wants with her friends, and stressed because if she hangs out with her friends, she has to monitor how she's talking to them.

As you will continue to learn, having those unwanted obsessions (as annoying, irritating, and frustrating as they are!) isn't what keeps the OCD episodes going. What feeds the OCD episodes is getting hooked on obsessions and responding to them with compulsions and escaping or avoidant behaviors, and ignoring your natural capacity to choose.

Don't worry if the difference between obsessions, compulsions, escaping, or avoidance is not crystal clear to you right now. Throughout the book you're going to learn in detail how to recognize each one of the components of the OCD package and learn skills to handle them while you continue to move forward with your life.

Let's move on to an activity to put into action what you just learned!

DO THIS!

Think about the different OCD episodes you experienced during the past week, choose one of them, and jot down each of the different components of the OCD episode as you see them. Again, no need to worry if it's not perfect, just give it your best shot!

Triggers	Obsessions
What are the triggers that start one of your OCD episodes? Is there anything you notice in your surroundings or internally—thoughts, images, urges—that starts the OCD episode?	What are the unwanted images, thoughts, and impulses that show up for you?
Compulsions	Avoidance/escape
What do you do to manage those annoying obsessions and make sure they don't become real?	What do you avoid to make sure those dark obsessions don't become real?

What are the short-term consequences of these compulsions and avoidance in your life?

What happens in the long term in your life because of these compulsions and avoidance behaviors?

Key question: What would you like to be doing more or less of if you weren't dealing with OCD episodes?

Now that you're getting familiar with the different components of an OCD episode, let's move into the Choice Point and how it applies to OCD.

CHAPTER 6

Getting Familiar with the Choice Point!

Here is a piece of reality: all of us, you, me, and everyone else, are constantly doing something. 24/7 we're watching YouTube videos, sending messages on Snapchat, scrolling through social media, writing, reading, laughing, thinking, daydreaming, hoping that our favorite TV show comes next, or even wishing for a mountain of dark chocolate! We don't go a single minute without doing something: even when taking a nap, we're doing something. There are things we do that others can see, like dancing, playing a sport, or eating, and then there is a bunch of stuff we do that is private. In our private moments, we're the only ones who know what we're pondering about, like the next movie we want to watch, the latest videogame that is coming out, or worrying about how much money is necessary for college.

The bottom line is that we're always doing something, regardless of whether we realize it or not, and sometimes that the things we do are steps towards creating a rich, fulfilling, and meaningful life, and other times, it's quite the opposite. Imagine, for a moment, living a life doing things that are not important to you or only doing things that others have pushed you into. Can you picture your life doing only things that feel meaningless? I'm sure that sometimes at school you think certain subjects are useless and that they won't help you in your life! But what about visualizing yourself doing less and less of the things you really want to do because of OCD episodes? That would be really hard, right?

In ACT, we pay close attention to the actions, behaviors, and concrete steps we do that move us toward the stuff we care about and those that take us away from the stuff we care about. And, here is where the Choice Point comes in handy, because it will help you *to keep an eye* on whether your actions, behaviors, and responses to those annoying obsessions are moving you towards or away from the stuff you care about day by day. It will constantly prompt you to choose what you really want to do instead of allowing the obsessions to boss you around. Chapter 14, "Choosing the Stuff You Care About!," will help you to explore more in detail what matters to you and to translate your values into specific actions.

Throughout the different sections in this workbook you will use the Choice Point graphic as a map to help you to do more of the things that matter to you. It will help you to remember that whenever those unwelcome obsessions show up, you can choose how to deal with them. When you're done with this workbook, you won't need to carry the Choice Point graphic with you at all times, because you will notice your Choice Points in your day-to-day life as those fears, anxieties, worries, and moments of uneasiness come your way, as they come to all of us in life. Let's begin!

KNOW THIS!

Here is what the Choice Point graphic looks like:

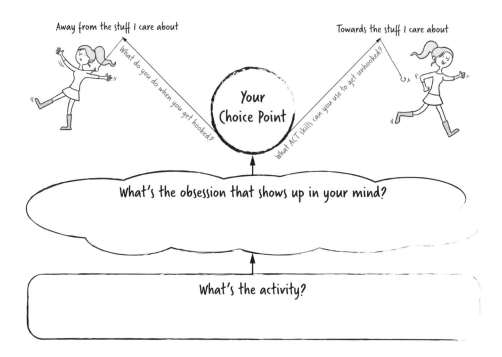

Let's break down the different parts of the Choice Point graphic so you can get familiar with it, since you will be using it throughout the book and in your quest to live your life to the full!

When working with the Choice Point graphic, we start from the bottom to the top. At the bottom of it, you are invited to identify a single thing: a specific activity you want to do and choose to do because it matters to you. It can be anything from playing sports, reading a book, hanging out with a friend, watching a movie, changing your hairstyle, and so on. Next, you have a bubble thought to write down all the obsessions that pop into your mind, like that little Chihuahua dog barking at you non-stop.

And at that point, as happens in real life, the Choice Point graphic reminds you that in any situation you're in, you have an opportunity to make a choice: you can choose to move towards the stuff you care about or away from it.

On the left side of the Choice Point graphic, you jot down all the things you do to suppress, minimize, distract, and get rid of those unsolicited obsessions that *get you hooked* and take you far away from the stuff that you care about, such as taking those dreadful obsessions as absolute truths, doing compulsions, or avoiding certain activities and people.

On the right side of the graphic, you write down all the skills or helpful pointers that you're going to learn in this workbook to *get unhooked* from those obsessions and take actions *toward* the stuff that is really important to you. Doable, right?

Additionally, it's often useful to write down the consequences of getting hooked on the obsessions above the phrase "Away from the stuff I care about."

The Choice Point graphic is not just a graphic, it also represents a moment in time, in your day-to-day life, in which you are reminded that you can put your choosing skills into action with courage, commitment, and energy, and live the life you want to live! The more you choose, the more you're likely to have an amazing, rich, and meaningful life, not a perfect life, but a life that is true to who you are.

As you move forward through the next chapters I encourage you to complete the Choice Point graphic over and over to practice doing the things that are important to you and plan your values-guided exposure practices. And, when you're done with this workbook, you can continue applying the Choice Point to your day-to-day life to make choices, live your personal values, and be the person you want to be!

When Norah from the previous chapter completed her Choice Point graphic, it looked like this:

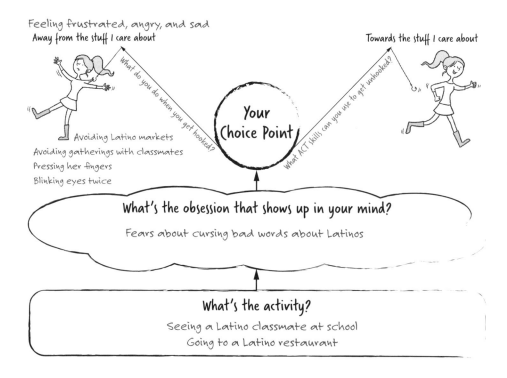

Feeling frustrated, angry, and sad
Away from the stuff I care about

Towards the stuff I care about

What do you do when you get hooked?

What ACT skills can you use to get unhooked?

Your Choice Point

Avoiding Latino markets
Avoiding gatherings with classmates
Pressing her fingers
Blinking eyes twice

What's the obsession that shows up in your mind?

Fears about cursing bad words about Latinos

What's the activity?

Seeing a Latino classmate at school
Going to a Latino restaurant

As you can see, Norah has been getting hooked on those pesky obsessions—and that's natural because she hasn't read this workbook yet!

TRY THIS!

If you were to complete your Choice Point graphic, how would that look like right now? Think of an activity you'd like to do that comes along with obsessions popping up in your mind.

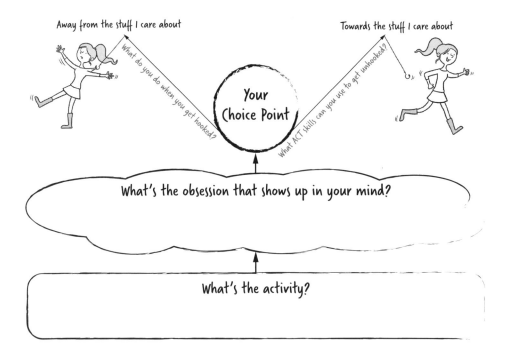

In the next section, you're going to study all those irritating obsessions that show up in your mind—in many different forms and shapes—so you can get better and better at recognizing them as creations of your mind and not as dictators of your behavior!

TAKEAWAYS!

You just finished reading the shortest section of the workbook and one of the most important ones because it introduced you to the Choice Point.

Here is what I learned over the years working with teens and their parents: no one likes to be told what to do, what to think, or what to feel! We all like to choose for ourselves, and the Choice Point brings to the forefront your natural capacity to choose not only how to handle the obsessions that show up in your mind, but also how to live your life moving forward!

At the end of the book, in the *Appendices*, you will find a blank Choice Point graphic so you can make copies and use it as needed. You can also download and print copies from www.jkp.com/catalogue/book/9781787750838, and remember, you can also check out the website www.actbeyondocd.com for the Choice Point and more resources.

MEETING THE "ANNOYING OBSESSIONS"

Did you know that we have approximately 5000 thoughts a day? Our minds get inundated with hundreds of doubts, questions, images, memories, hypotheses, requests, problems to solve, ideas about trips to take, reminders of movies we want to watch, worries, dreams, and so much more stuff, every single day without exception.

For instance, right now, while I'm typing on the computer, my mind has wandering thoughts about my cat, my mom's medication, my sister's trip, my students, whether you will like this workbook or not, and so on—my mind is in full motion. What about your mind? If you pause for three minutes in this moment and just watch what your mind comes up with before continuing to read this paragraph, what does your mind do? What did you notice?

It's part of our make up as human beings: we have busy minds and they come with us wherever we go. Wherever we are, there is our mind chatting, chatting, and chatting some more. Is it really possible that every single thought is important to us? And is it really necessary to answer, entertain, or respond to all the thoughts, memories, and images that show up in our mind constantly? Quite likely no, as otherwise, our days would be dedicated to managing our mind as a full-time job. Some thoughts are really important—like the thought about the essay you have to write or the chemistry formula for the upcoming quiz you have to take—but other thoughts are just pure mind noise because they don't drive any action, are insignificant, and they actually distract you from what you are supposed to be doing in a given moment.

In this section you're going to study the obsessions you're struggling with, one by one, so you can get better and better at catching them on-the-fly and choosing your response to them!

CHAPTER 7

Unwanted Annoying Thoughts

Anya, a 16-year-old, was in charge of organizing the schedule for the annual camping trip with her high school classmates. She was excited and ready to make phone calls and gather prices for transportation, camping sites, etc., but in the middle of preparing for those errands she noticed a red stain on the hardwood floor of her house. Quickly her mind came up with the thought, "Did I step on it? What if it's blood? What if I get an illness? Is it fresh blood?" Immediately, Anya jumped in the shower and washed her feet as carefully as possible in case her socks got contaminated and touched her skin. Afterwards, Anya ended up throwing away her shoes.

Anya had unwanted thoughts about getting contaminated: What if I get an illness? What if I get contaminated? Indeed, it's very distressing for anyone to have their mind come up with that thought, but Anya's mind was playing tricks with her. And because that obsession came along with so much fear, she got hooked on it and took it as the absolute truth. Immediately afterwards, she started doing a bunch of stuff to make sure she didn't get contaminated or ill.

KNOW THIS!

Obsessions are so distressing when they show up because they come so abruptly, are repetitive, and are uncomfortable to have. Remember that this happens because your brain is in overdrive, identifying anything and everything that could potentially hurt you.

The fact is that—naturally and without being asked—your mind will come up with many, many thoughts, images, weird stuff, and fun stuff, 24/7, nonstop, because that's what minds do. Your mind, my mind, and everyone else's minds are constantly coming up with all types of content like a *content generator machine* because they have been trained to do that since people lived in caves.

Our task is not to change our minds. We can't just buy a new mind at the grocery store! Instead, our task is to learn to recognize when we're getting hooked and taking our thoughts too seriously and to choose helpful thoughts versus noise ones, and to recognize obsessions as objects our content generator machine comes up with, rather than taking them seriously and as the absolute truth.

Moving onward, instead of checking whether your obsessions are real, you're going learn to catch them and take them as they are: just thoughts, bouncing in your mind like soap bubbles.

DO THIS!

Think about the last month and, for this activity, jot down inside the cloud all the unwanted obsessive thoughts that the content generator machine of your mind came up with. Maybe there is only one, or a couple, or many, but just do the best you can to recall those annoying obsessions that were showing up over and over in your mind! Anya's thought bubble looks like this:

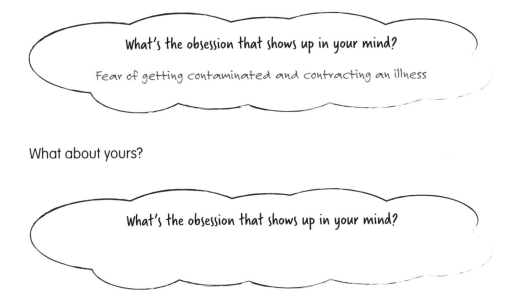

What's the obsession that shows up in your mind?

Fear of getting contaminated and contracting an illness

What about yours?

What's the obsession that shows up in your mind?

TRY THIS!

This week, if you find your mind comes up with intrusive thoughts, catch them with the Choice Point graphic as people do on a fishing trip when catching a fish in a net.

You can practice catching those obsessions at the end of the day or, if you have a piece of paper and a pen to hand, you can draw your own Choice Point with your personal touch. Either way, jot down at the bottom of it the situation or activity you were doing in that moment of the OCD episode, and, inside the thought bubble, write down all the annoying obsessions that showed up then. Noticing the obsessions is a core skill. Remember, obsessions are the unwanted, unsolicited, and annoying thoughts that show up. Compulsions on the other hand are everything you do to control, suppress, and neutralize the obsession right away.

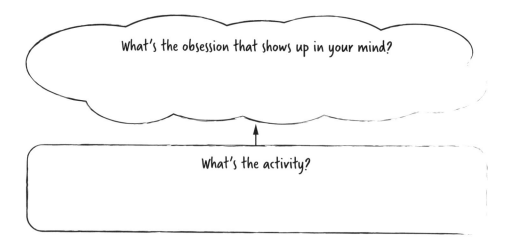

The more you practice, the better you will get at noticing your obsessions, which will allow you to choose how to respond when those intrusive thoughts show up, instead of getting hooked on them.

CHAPTER 8

Unsolicited Bizarre Images

Mike grew up in the Jewish community and it was very important for him to live according to the principles of his faith. However, one day he was participating in the service, and while listening to the pastor, he shook his head as if something was wrong. He had a very scary image pop up in his mind about becoming a villain in a superhero movie. Mike shook his head again trying to make the image go away, but to his surprise, he could still see this image very clearly in his mind. He got anxious, scared, and petrified that this villain image was his true self; he tried to continue listening to the service but he couldn't let go of this horrible image. Mike felt so bad about it because he liked attending services, liked participating in the youth group, and was a big fan of the rabbi. Yet, he started doubting himself over and over about whether he was pursuing his faith or not.

Have you guessed what was going on with Mike? He had an obsession—he totally got hooked on the horrible image of becoming a villain and got scared about not living up to his faith. For Mike, this was very sad, because if he considered it objectively, it was evident that he really embraced his faith as best he could. Yet, his mind, as the typical content generator machine we all carry with us, was doing its job by coming up with all types of nonsensical stuff at the speed of light, and on this day it came up with the unwanted image Mike had. Let's go over this in a bit of more detail in the rest of this chapter.

KNOW THIS!

Obsessions are not just thoughts or sentences, they can also be intrusive images that are unwanted, bizarre, nonsensical, and show up out of the blue. Most of my clients are usually surprised and relieved to know that those scary images are intrusions or obsessions: consider Jacquie, a woman who just delivered her first child and had an image of dropping her baby from the balcony even though she was extremely excited about becoming a mom; or Justin, who after watching a scary movie had the image of using his car to hurt his parents, even though he loved them very much and would never hurt them.

Everyone, including myself, has annoying images like that from time to time, because our minds are skillful at generating tons of content. But if you take those images as absolute truths or possibilities, get hooked on their content, and forget that you can choose how to respond to them, then you easily end up responding with compulsions and escaping or avoidance behaviors that are time-consuming, use up your energy, and stop you from living life to the full.

DO THIS!

Does the *content generator machine* of your mind come up with any obsessive images that are totally unwanted, distressing, and unexpected? If so, do your best to answer the questions in the form below. If not, I would still invite you to take a quick peek at the questions below so you continue to get familiar with OCD.

Where were you? With whom? What time of the day?

What started the OCD episode?

What was the unwanted image that came up in your mind? Can you draw it? If not, just write it down.

TRY THIS!

Take some time to think about OCD episodes at the end of every day, grab your Choice Point graphic, and start from the bottom as usual, writing down what activity you were doing, and write down those unwelcomed images that your mind came up with in the thought bubble. Keep in mind that writing them down is not about challenging them as real or not, accurate or not, but just noticing them, catching them, and seeing them for what they are: obnoxious images your overworking brain is coming up with.

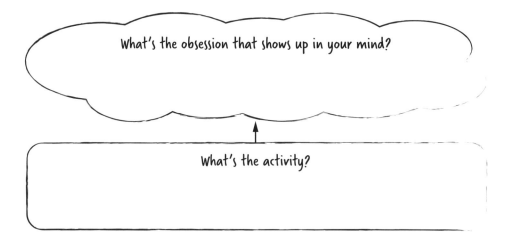

What's the obsession that shows up in your mind?

What's the activity?

Remember that obsessions, as domineering as they may look, are going to pop up now and again, because that's what our minds do. But learning to catch them is going to help you to handle OCD episodes more effectively so you can move along with your day!

CHAPTER 9

Uninvited Urges

Izzy, a gender nonconforming teen, was hanging out at their friend's house, and while talking about an upcoming music concert, they suddenly had an intense urge to start cursing and yelling derogatory names at their friends. The urge to do these mean things was so strong that Izzy felt that they were really going to do them, and that the only way to control it was to cover their mouth quickly and stop talking to their friends. Izzy felt petrified at the idea of offending their friends, felt embarrassed and sad about what happened, and quickly decided to leave the gathering to make sure they didn't hurt their friends.

Izzy was dealing with obsessions, but these ones weren't in the form of thoughts or images, as discussed in the previous chapters. Instead, they took the form of an impulse, urge, or rush that Izzy felt and took as the absolute truth without knowing that it was an obsession and not a mandate to act. Isn't that interesting how obsessions have different forms?

KNOW THIS!

People who don't know about OCD often think that obsessions are only related to thoughts, catastrophic endings, or bizarre images, but obsessions also refer to nonsensical urges, impulses, or rushes like Izzy had.

Here is another example for you:

Mark, a client of mine, was walking on the Golden Gate Bridge in San Francisco, a very high bridge that people like to visit as a tourist site because of its amazing view of the city. While he was walking and enjoying the view, totally out of the blue, he felt a strong feeling, like an urge or impulse, that he was going to jump from the bridge. Mark got scared about those urges, and the content generator machine of his mind quickly came up with thoughts like "What if I jump? What if I really want to jump? If I feel this, does it mean I want to commit suicide?" In reality, Mark didn't want to kill or harm himself, he was enjoying his trip, was on vacation, and even though his life wasn't perfect, he really liked his school, had good friends, and he cared for his family.

If you're dealing with obsessions that are more like urges, you might be afraid that you're going to act on those urges, impulses, rushes, or strong sensations just because you have them, as if having an urge is the same as acting on it. This strong feeling, like you're being pushed to do something that you really don't want to do, is an annoying obsession, but having these urges or impulses doesn't mean that they will make you do things you don't want to do.

At the end of the day, urges, impulses, and rushes are just that: urges, impulses, and rushes that we experience. It is just that your mind is playing tricks again and working extra hard perceiving those urges as dangerous!

If you like playing sports, or even if you don't play sports but you run up and down the stairs at home or at school, you may notice that your body has strong reactions: your breathing gets heavy, the temperature of your body changes, your heart starts beating faster, and so on. But you don't *do* much with those physical sensations in that particular situation, you just have them, right?

In this workbook, you're going to learn to have obsessions, like urges, in the same way as you have strong physical reactions at other times, and to choose your response to them. These are reactions and experiences your body has and goes through, and you don't need to do anything about them or give them any more attention than they deserve!

DO THIS!

For this exercise, think back over the last three months and recall an occasion where you felt stuck in an OCD episode and found it hard to let go of the obsession and move on with your day. Was there a particular urge, rush, or impulse you felt about doing something that you actually didn't want to do, didn't make sense to you, and yet you felt scared about taking action on it? If so, then complete the sentences below. If not, take another look at those difficult OCD episodes and see if there was any other in which the obsession was an urge or an impulse, as if you felt like doing something that you actually didn't want to do. If you still don't experience obsessive urges, take a quick look at the questions below so you continue to get familiar with how obsessions show up.

The most common obsessive urges that showed up for me are:

_____

_____

_____

_____

_____

And usually, when they show up, I do the following:

_____

_____

_____

_____

_____

_____

Little by little you're going to get better and better at catching your obsessive urges and any other obsession that comes your way. This is an important step towards choosing a helpful way to handle them.

TRY THIS!

For this coming week, make time in your schedule to grab your Choice Point graphic at the end of each day, or draw your own, and check if you have any obsessive urges showing up. By now, you're familiar with completing the bottom part of the Choice Point—about the activity and the obsession—so I won't repeat the directions for it. If you do have any questions about how to complete this portion of the Choice Point graphic, just take a look back at the previous chapter and get the answers from there.

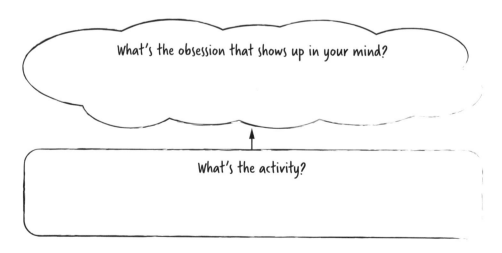

What's the obsession that shows up in your mind?

What's the activity?

Before moving to the next section, here is my last tip for you: as challenging as it is having a hardworking mind and a very busy content generator machine, it doesn't mean you cannot get unhooked and cannot choose how to respond to those pesky obsessions.

That's what this workbook is really about—helping you to choose how to handle those obsessions or any uncomfortable experience you go through, so you can move forward in your life. Little by little, step-by-step, in all these chapters, you will be able to catch an obsession as it is, at any time, experience it, and put your choosing skills into action!

ACTIVITY

How about completing this word scramble with key words from this section?

    1. SINSOSEOBS _____

    2. FERA _____

    3. UGSER _____

    4. SSBIEESVO IMASGE _____

    5. EDUNATNW TSOGHUHT _____

Find the answers in Appendix 7.

TAKEAWAYS!

You just learned that obsessions—as annoying as they are—are just a form of mind noise. By nature, obsessions come and go, sometimes faster, sometimes slower, but they're pushy and sticky, and demand that you pay attention to them all the time. While you continue working on this workbook, I want to invite you to ponder this question: Do you really have to respond to the train of obsessions that show up in your mind and do whatever they say in those moments? I cannot answer that question for you, but I want to strongly invite you to think about it as you move along with your day.

As simple as it sounds, noticing your obsessions on-the-fly, as they come, really is the beginning of shifting your relationship with them and how you handle them in your day-to-day living. Do your best to catch them as they come! Keep going!

ARE YOU HOOKED?

You made it to a new section! Kudos to you!

Let's be real: Nobody likes to have obsessions! No matter how many times your parents or psychologists tell you that "it's okay to have those obsessions, they're normal," it's still upsetting and challenging. I've never heard any of my clients saying, "I love it when these annoying images show up." It's quite the opposite. Most of my clients get irritated when having them, find them distressful, and, understandably, they, like you, do everything they can to handle them the best they can—sometimes effectively, sometimes not.

In this section, you're going to learn in detail about specific strategies you may be using to manage obsessions, such as compulsions, avoidance, and reassurance-seeking behaviors that, in the moment, may help you to feel less anxious, less scared, and less panicky. But, as we've learnt, in the long-term those strategies are the ones that keep you hooked on an obsession, sucking away your energy like vampires, and taking you in the opposite direction of the stuff you care about in your day-to-day life.

Let's begin!

CHAPTER 10

Buying Tickets to Compulsion City!

Do you know where "Compulsion City" is located on a world map? After reading this question, have you searched for the answer to it on Google? Have you texted your friend asking about it? Let me save you some time, because you won't find this country on a map. But, if you look at all the things you do to neutralize, fight back, or push away your pesky obsessions, it's possible that you have transported yourself to Compulsion City!

Obsessions are annoying creatures that the content generator of your mind throws at you, because as you know by now, that's what our brain does! And when encountering a triggering situation, in that precise moment, you may do everything you can to get rid of the obsessions, minimize the fear that comes along with them, and push away any chance for those obsessions to become real. Those behaviors are called compulsions, and you read about them in previous chapters. Now, we're going to zoom into them. Ready?

Let's begin with an example:

> Rihanna, a 16-year-old, was dealing with an obsession of getting cancer after visiting her aunt at the hospital. As soon as she held her aunt's hand, she had this thought: "Am I going to get cancer like my aunt? Will I be as sick as she is? Did I get my aunt's cancer?" Rihanna knew that she couldn't get cancer from giving a hug to her aunt or holding her hand, and yet, she ended up doing the following behaviors: asking

in a health forum whether she could get cancer, checking Wikipedia, googling for hours about how people get cancer, asking her parents about it, washing her hands multiple times, telling herself over and over, "I'm going to be okay, it's not possible to get cancer from holding her hand," and repeating in her mind her lucky numbers 2, 4, and 6 every time she had this thought. All those behaviors that Rihanna did to make sure she didn't get cancer are compulsions.

Now, let's take a look at how you handle those irritating obsessions when they show up for you. In the form below, list all the things you do to manage the unwanted obsessions that pop up in your mind when feeling triggered. Do your best to list all of them so you can prepare yourself for putting into action choosing skills later on. First things first, right?

What are all the things you have tried to make sure those obsessions go away and don't come back your way? Do your best to list all the things you do. Don't worry how short or long the list looks, just make sure to write as specifically as possible all those strategies you do to handle your obsessions, even if they may seem insignificant or silly.

After you have listed all the strategies you use to manage your obsessions, make a circle around the compulsions. Remember that *compulsions are all those things you do, right away,* when triggered with an obsession in order to reduce the unpleasant feelings that come along with the obsessions. Just to clarify, watching movies for six hours on a Monday evening looks like a strategy to manage OCD, but it's not necessarily a behavior that happens right away at the moment an obsession shows up. Compulsions are those things that you do immediately, as soon as an obsession pops up, and as soon as you do them, the fear, anxiety, panic, and all the discomfort go down. Do you see the difference? There are many other things you may do to manage OCD in general—watching TV, avoiding going to school, and so on—but compulsions are the things you do right there, when the intrusive thoughts show up.

You may wonder, why is it important to recognize your compulsions if you already know that OCD is annoying? Here is my short response for you: *If you're not aware of your compulsions, you will miss your Choice Point when having an obsession. And if you're not aware of your Choice Point, you cannot move in the direction of the things that you care about.*

KNOW THIS!

Let's focus in a bit more on compulsions, so you can get better and better at recognizing them and continue to build your choosing skills!

Compulsions can be overt, public, or observable by others, or they can be private or mental, so nobody sees them. For instance, Rihanna telling herself, "I'm going to be okay, it's not possible I will get cancer," and repeating her lucky numbers 2, 4, and 6, are private or mental compulsions because no one can see them—she's the only one that knows about these thoughts. But, when she searches for information on Google, asks her parents, or washes her hands to make sure she doesn't contract cancer, those are called public or overt compulsions because they're observable by others.

Here is a summary of Rihanna's public and private compulsions:

Overt compulsions (public)	Covert compulsions (private)
Checking on Wikipedia Asking Google Asking her parents Washing her hands	Telling herself "I won't get cancer" Repeating her lucky numbers 2, 4, and 6

One little extra thing for you to know about compulsions: if the compulsions are always done in the same way, they're called ritualized compulsions—like when Rihanna repeats the same order when saying her lucky numbers. But, when the compulsions are completed in a different order, or repeated at random number of times or until they feel right, they're called non-ritualized compulsions.

Let's take a more detailed look into ritualized and non-ritualized compulsions in Rihanna's behaviors. When Rihanna repeats her lucky numbers 2, 4, and 6, she usually does it three times every time. When washing her hands, she does it in the same manner: turning on the faucet, letting the water run for 20 seconds, pumping the liquid soap on her hands, rubbing the top of each hand while counting until 30, and then washing them with water while counting for 60 seconds. These are ritualized compulsions because they're done in the same order every time. If the compulsion is not done in the same way, then we describe those compulsions as non-ritualized.

Sometimes, compulsions are tricky to catch because they seem like regular behaviors that everyone does. For example, double-checking your answers when completing a test seems to be a natural behavior that any student will do, right? However, if you're dealing with OCD, you want to pay careful attention to what happens to your anxiety, fear, and panic reactions when you double-check your responses on a test and be clear about your reasons for doing so. If you do this particular behavior to make sure your obsession or fearful thoughts about getting answers wrong don't become true and your discomfort decreases right away, almost immediately, then chances are that double-checking your answers when taking a test is a compulsion. And, as you're learning, compulsions are one of those behaviors that feed OCD, all the way.

DO THIS!

For this activity, list in the form below all the compulsions you do when getting hooked on an annoying obsession.

What overt or public compulsions do you do to manage obsessions?	What covert or private compulsions do you do to manage obsessions?

Afterwards, draw a circle around any ritualized compulsions.

TRY THIS!

Take some time this week to practice recognizing those compulsive responses. If you have an OCD episode, make sure to jot down at the end of the day how you got hooked on that particular obsession and the compulsions that came along with it. Because compulsions get you hooked, remember to write them down on the left side of the Choice Point graphic.

When Rihanna completed her Choice Point graphic, it looked like this:

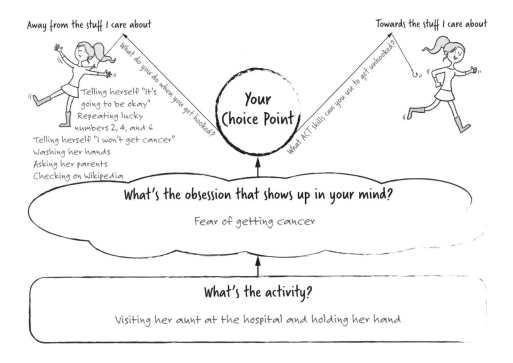

Away from the stuff I care about

Towards the stuff I care about

What do you do when you get hooked?

What ACT skills can you use to get unhooked?

Your Choice Point

Telling herself "It's going to be okay"
Repeating lucky numbers 2, 4, and 6
Telling herself "I won't get cancer"
Washing her hands
Asking her parents
Checking on Wikipedia

What's the obsession that shows up in your mind?

Fear of getting cancer

What's the activity?

Visiting her aunt at the hospital and holding her hand

Your turn!

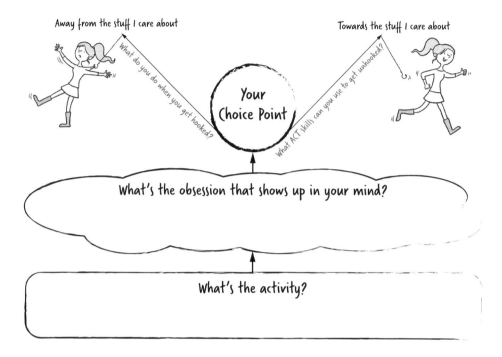

Now that you have checked all the compulsions you rely on to discard, suppress, and control your obsessions, let's take a look at another type of behavior you may use when dealing with annoying obsessions: avoidant behaviors.

CHAPTER 11

Running as Fast as You Can to Avoidance City

As you know, even when you try really hard to get rid of obsessions, they keep showing up, and sometimes it's just one after another. Naturally, you do what you can to manage them. Sometimes, you rely on compulsions, and at other times, you put on the fastest running shoes you have to run away from a triggering situation—and you run straight to *Avoidance City*.

KNOW THIS!

Going back to the example of Rihanna from Chapter 10, sometimes she gets so anxious, fearful, and uncomfortable that she comes up with all types of reasons to avoid visiting her aunt at the hospital, like having to do homework or feeling a bit sick. Other times, Rihanna turns the radio or the TV off when there is news about cancer or anything related to it. All those behaviors are named "escaping" or "avoidance," and while they're very handy for Rihanna because they make her anxiety decrease really quickly, she ends up missing time with her aunt, feels bad for not visiting her, and gets far away from being the caring person she wants to be.

Rihanna will definitely benefit from learning to step back and find her Choice Point in those moments, and to remember that she can choose how to respond to those obsessions instead of getting bossed around by them.

DO THIS!

Let's start by listing all the things you do to avoid going through the fear and discomfort that comes along with those annoying obsessions. Don't worry about if your list is long or short, just do your best to note down all the things you avoid, including people, situations, and activities.

What situations, people, places, activities, and stuff do you like to do but have avoided because of your obsessions?

Rihanna's response: I like to spend time with my aunt but have avoided going to visit her at the hospital.

I like spending time with my mom but I avoid giving her a hug after she's back from the hospital.

I like watching Tv but can't take listening to news stories about cancer, so avoid them.

How do you feel after listing all the things you have been avoiding? Hang in there! The more aware you are of how you get hooked with obsessions, the more skillful you're going to be at getting unhooked and moving forward doing what's important to you!

And just to clarify, I'm not saying that all avoidant behaviors are bad or wrong: we all avoid certain things at times. For example, when I'm driving on the freeway and I see something that may look like a dead animal, I do avoid looking because I'm an animal lover and it's hard for me to see those images. This is an avoidant behavior, but my life doesn't get narrower and narrower because of it. I'm able to continue seeing my clients and be the daughter, friend, and partner I want to be. Now, imagine that I had a panic attack when driving and it was so scary that I ended up not driving to work the next day, and as my fear progressed, I began to avoid driving to the grocery store or the pet store. Would you say that my avoidant behaviors are a move towards or away from my personal values? They're a move away, because I won't be the caring person I want to be with my family, clients, and pets.

Sometimes you may decide to avoid certain things, and that's human. But I do want to invite you to check carefully whether those moves are taking you closer to be the person you want to be or not.

TRY THIS!

At the end of every day this week, think about any OCD episodes from that day, check for yourself if you reacted with any escaping or avoidant behaviors, and, if so, jot them down in the Choice Point graphic.

Important tip: The more you track your behavior, the more chances you give yourself to find your own Choice Point in those moments of struggle. We all get lost at some point, but we get lost because we don't know where we're walking.

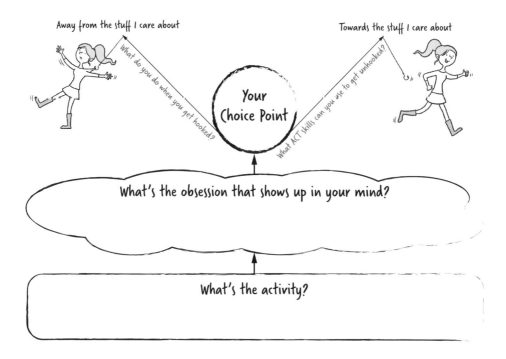

Away from the stuff I care about

Towards the stuff I care about

What do you do when you get hooked?

Your Choice Point

What ACT skills can you use to get unhooked?

What's the obsession that shows up in your mind?

What's the activity?

CHAPTER 12

Asking for Accommodations

Jonathan: Mom, are you sure these shoes are good? I wore them last week, and I'm not sure if I can wear them again.

Mom: Jon, I told you four times already—those are good shoes, they look good on you, and people wear the same shoes all the time.

Jonathan: Mom, I just don't know, because last week they didn't feel right, and I don't want to mess up my day today.

Mom: Jon, it's going to be okay. Nothing bad is going to happen.

Jonathan: Mom, I don't know. Can you please put these shoes outside and make sure they don't touch anything we bring into the house?

Mom: Here we are again with those requests. Fine—as long as you go to school. Sure, I'll put these shoes outside. Just make sure you go to school today. You cannot miss school!

Jonathan, a 14-year-old, has been struggling with mixing things with bad energy with things with good energy. For example, when he had a bad day at school—whether because he got a bad grade, didn't know how to answer a question, the weather felt different, or a friend got upset with him—he was afraid of causing harm to himself by mixing items he wore that day—when he had negative experiences—with new experiences on a new day. And to make sure he was going to be safe, Jonathan asked his mom multiple times if he was going to be okay, and kept doing it until she answered the question with the "right feeling." When her answer didn't feel right, he asked his mom to make an accommodation for him, to put the shoes outside of the house. His mom wanted him to go to school and to not miss a day, so naturally, she did what would "help" Jonathan—in the moment—so he could attend school.

But, let's step back for a second. Every time his mom put the shoes outside, put specific pieces of clothing in plastic bags so they wouldn't touch Jonathan's clothes, changed her clothes before he started getting anxious, or cleaned her cell phone from "bad energy," and so on, Jon's fear about getting hurt by mixing good and bad energies decreases right away. But it only decreases until he gets triggered again, and a new OCD episode starts, and the cycle repeats, again and again. Any reactions when reading this?

Jon is definitely struggling and feels scared, nervous, and panicky when getting hooked on his intrusive thoughts about bringing harm to himself. He quickly takes that obsession as an absolute fact, and because it feels so real, he *feels* he must do something to decrease his fear: he asks his mom to change her behavior. Those requests to others—to do something or to stop doing something, or any other request to modify their behavior—are called asking for accommodations.

KNOW THIS!

Accommodations are requests you make to others—parents, caregivers, friends, or anyone else—to reduce the anxiety, panic, and distress that come along with the uninvited obsession that pops up in your mind. Accommodations can vary from asking whoever drives you to school to drive you back home because you're too anxious, asking your friends to move some things for you so you don't contaminate items, or demanding that everyone follows your directions at home about washing their hands in a particular way, just to name a few examples.

DO THIS!

What about checking for yourself if you're requesting any type of accommodation to manage those unsolicited obsessions that the content generator machine of your brain comes up with? Do your best to list below all those people you have asked for accommodations when you are feeling triggered by intrusive thoughts.

Who do you make special requests to when having an obsession?	What type of accommodation do you ask for?	What would happen if that person didn't go along with your request for accommodations?
Example: Ryan, my classmate in history class.	Can you put the chemistry book apart from the history one please?	I'll be scared of mixing bad energies from the chemistry class with the history class. It will feel wrong, as if something really bad could happen to me.

Now that you have recognized the accommodations you asked others to do for you, here are two more questions for you:

What happens to your fear, discomfort, or anxiety when a person makes an accommodation?

_____

_____

_____

_____

_____

_____

And if you look at your day-to-day life, do those accommodations really help you to do the things you want to do and live the life you want to live, or do they keep feeding into OCD episodes?

_____

_____

_____

_____

_____

_____

TRY THIS!

Everything you're learning in this workbook is a skill to put into action so you can get better and better at living your life while carrying those obsessions along with you. Looking back at last week or month, think about the three most common requests for accommodations you have made and jot them down in the Choice Point graphic. Check for yourself again—are those requests you make moving you away from or towards living your life to the fullest? No one better than you to check! If there are moves away, make sure to write them down where they belong, on the left side of the Choice Point graphic.

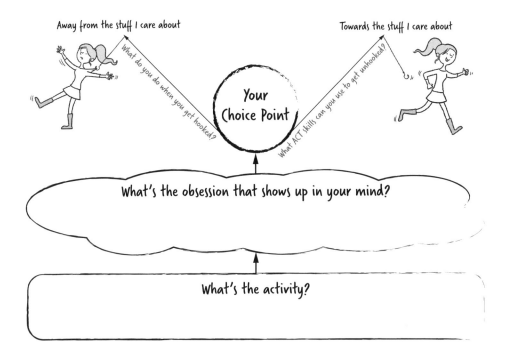

Away from the stuff I care about

Towards the stuff I care about

What do you do when you get hooked?

What ACT skills can you use to get unhooked?

Your Choice Point

What's the obsession that shows up in your mind?

What's the activity?

CHAPTER 13

Checking the Costs of Getting Hooked

Engaging in compulsions and avoidant behaviors, or asking for accommodations from others from time to time, is natural—we all do all types of things when our mind comes up with very annoying stuff and we feel scared.

But because this is a book about OCD, and even though I don't know you, I have a strong sense that you have been trying hard, really hard, to manage, control, and figure out how to solve the *obsession problem*. How about we take a look at how all these behaviors really work in your battle with obsessions?

KNOW THIS!

Over and over in this workbook you will be asked a very important question: Do compulsive behaviors, avoidant behaviors, and asking for accommodations from others take you closer to becoming the person you want to be or further away?

Notice that I'm not asking if these behaviors—compulsions, avoidance, or asking for accommodations—are reasonable, justifiable, accurate, true or false, or anything like that, because chances are that when trying to answer those questions, you will get hooked on your obsessions and trapped into your mind very quickly!

It's possible that you may already be spending hours and hours trying to solve an unsolvable problem from the content generator of your mind when having obsessions. But, reality is that there is no winning a battle with an overworking brain sending you tons of danger signals because it will come back quickly with new content, push you to do more compulsions, demand you avoid a situation, and encourage you to ask for accommodations. Believe it or not, your brain is just trying to protect you. And it's doing exactly what it's supposed to be doing, as my brain and everyone else's brain does too.

For example, going back to Jonathan from the last chapter who was "asking for accommodations," with time he realized that asking his mom for accommodations was another way of getting hooked onto obsessions. The short-term relief was temporary. In the end, it didn't help Jonathan to do the things he cared about, like riding his bike, participating in the swimming team, spending time with his family, or simply enjoying small things like having a vegan chocolate donut. Jonathan was too busy taking his obsession of bad things happening to him as a result of attracting bad energy too seriously and seeking temporary relief from his distress.

And if you recall Rihanna, from Chapters 10 and 11, "Buying Tickets to Compulsion City!" and "Running as Fast as You Can to Avoidance City," her compulsive behaviors—telling herself "it's going to be okay," repeating her lucky numbers, washing her hands—and avoidant behaviors—avoiding visiting her aunt, hugging her mom, or listening to news related to cancer— always worked in the short term because they helped Rihanna to quickly manage the yucky feeling that comes with obsessions.

But, going back to the initial question of this section: Do compulsions, avoidant behaviors, and asking for accommodations to others take you closer to becoming the person you want to be or further away? What would you say? Most of my clients would say *No!!!!! They work always in the heat of the moment, but then I'm back to the hundreds of OCD episodes that come after that*. All these behaviors can be risky in the long run, right? It's like all those behaviors take you into safety country!

You may have already figured that out, but keeping in mind that this workbook is about teaching you to live flexibly with all those fearful, distressing, and frightful moments that come in life, let me make it crystal clear that avoidance, compulsions, and accommodations are natural human responses for you, for me, and for everyone around us. It's only when we use them in automatic pilot mode, when unsolicited obsessions show up frequently, and with the purpose of minimizing our distress right away that they backfire, feed into OCD episodes, and consume your enthusiasm and energy until you don't have anything left over to do the stuff you care about.

All the teens I've worked with want to get rid of their obsessions, and they try really hard, as much as you do. Nothing works well until they find their Choice Point to pause, regroup, and choose their responses before engaging in compulsions, avoidant behaviors, or asking others for accommodations. You can do it too!

DO THIS!

Can you answer some questions about how all these behavioral responses play out in your day-to-day life?

1. What happens right away with those fearful obsessions when you visit Compulsion City or its neighbor, Escape City? Do they get better, worse, or do they stay the same?

_____

_____

_____

_____

_____

_____

2. What happens when you try to prove with logic that the obsessions are wrong, inaccurate, or mistaken?

_____

_____

_____

_____

_____

_____

3. Run through your mind an entire week when you were dealing with the annoying obsessions your mind came up with, recall the compulsions you engaged in, and then complete the following with how long you spend on each compulsion:

Compulsion: _____ Hours: _____ Minutes: _____

Compulsion: _____ Hours: _____ Minutes: _____

Compulsion: _____ Hours: _____ Minutes: _____

Compulsion: _____ Hours: _____ Minutes: _____

Compulsion: _____ Hours: _____ Minutes: _____

Compulsion: _____ Hours: _____ Minutes: _____

Compulsion: _____ Hours: _____ Minutes: _____

Compulsion: _____ Hours: _____ Minutes: _____

Compulsion: _____ Hours: _____ Minutes: _____

If I choose the 10 most frequent compulsions I get stuck on, I spend an average of _____ (total number of hours and minutes) a day.

4. Think about the stuff that you actually care about but ended up avoiding because the obsessions were in full motion in your mind.

a. _____

b. _____

c. _____

d. _____

e. _____

5. Can you describe the ways in which OCD episodes have affected your life?

a. In my friendships OCD episodes have affected me by:

_____

_____

_____

_____

_____

_____

b. At school, OCD episodes have upset me by:

_____

_____

_____

_____

_____

_____

c. At home, OCD episodes have affected me by:

_____

_____

_____

_____

_____

_____

d. In my hobbies, OCD episodes have influenced me to:

_____

_____

_____

_____

_____

e. In regard to myself, OCD episodes have led me to:

_____

_____

_____

_____

_____

Any reactions when looking at the sentences you just completed? What about answering one final question?

What's the long-term effect on your day-to-day life of doing compulsions, engaging in avoidant behaviors, and requesting accommodations from others?

_____

_____

_____

_____

_____

We both know that you have tried very hard to handle those obsessions, to the best you can, and yet, look at all the consequences you have encountered over the long term—it's tough, isn't it?

And if you step back, it all happens because an uninvited, annoying, unwanted obsession shows up in your mind and you spent too much time *living with it rather than having it.* You cannot choose which obsessions, thoughts, images, memories, doubtful thoughts, fantasy thoughts, or future thoughts come to your mind, they just happen. Imagine for a second that those obsessions are like balls in a swimming pool that contain all the uncanny images, urges, and thoughts you don't like, don't want, and don't need, but they're there...floating and floating in the pool. Because you don't like them, you push them down with both hands, and you push them down again as hard as possible, and you make sure that those balls are below the water. For a moment it seems that you have succeeded. You cannot see the balls carrying your obsessions because you are holding them down, but the next thing you know, the moment you lift your hands, they bounce back with more force, one after another, and when you look at the pool you see all of them there, exactly where they were before, floating.

Would you say that maybe pushing, fighting against, arguing back, replacing them, and basically spending all your effort and energy on stopping those obsessions and living in safety country is just not working at all? Does living in safety country keep you busy, too busy to do the things you really care about? Are all those efforts from Compulsion City and Avoidance City, and all those requests for accommodations, helpful to you in being the person you want to be?

Let's step back for a moment. Are you up for an experiment? Let's see. Do your best to follow these directions:

1. For the next couple of moments, try as hard as possible to not imagine your best friend.

2. Don't visualize your favorite music band.

3. Don't think about your school.

4. And lastly, give your best shot at not picturing your favorite video game.

What happened when you did this experiment? I know that for me the more that I try to not imagine, visualize, remember, recall, or think of anything, the more I have those images, thoughts, memories, etc.

Tough, huh? Think about all the times you tried to push down those obsessions like the balls in a swimming pool, what was the real outcome?

Obsessions pop and pop, float and float, swim and swim, like balls in a pool, because that's just what the content generator device of your mind does at all times, non-stop, 24/7, no holidays, and no vacation. If all your efforts to push down, suppress, get rid of, and eliminate only work for a couple of seconds, and in the long run, all the short-term pay offs backfire in your life, what about trying something different, like choosing and doing what you care about with your feet, hands, and mouth?

TRY THIS!

Use your Choice Point graphic for the following. This week, when you notice an OCD episode, see if you can reflect what you do when getting hooked on obsessions. After jotting down the situation in which it happened and the obsession that came up in your mind, jot down on top of the phrase "Away from the stuff I care about" how OCD has affected your day. Here is an example of how the Choice Point graphic looks:

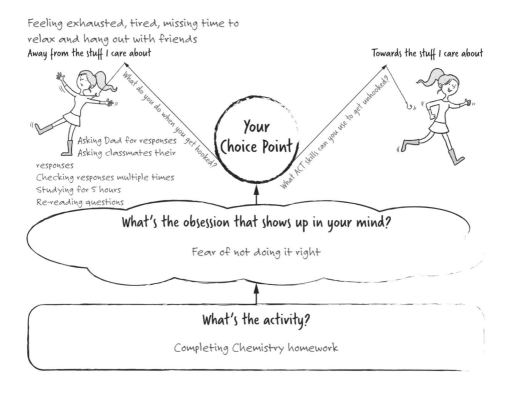

What about yours?

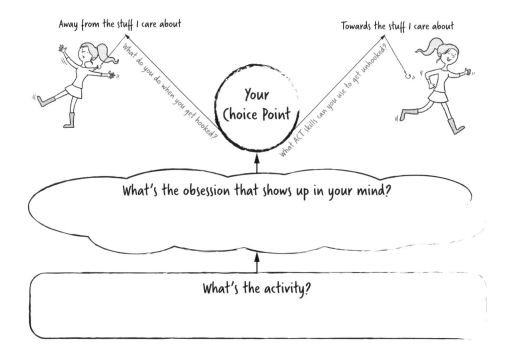

Remember, the more you practice catching OCD and its impact on your life, the better you're going to get at unhooking from those annoying obsessions and getting out of safety country.

TAKEAWAYS!

Great work! You just finished a very important section in this workbook and in your journey towards getting unhooked from pesky obsessions and back into your life.

In this section you learned that having an obsession, as annoying as it is, is not what leads to an OCD episode. Rather, it's the compulsive, avoidant, and reassurance-seeking behaviors that feed an OCD episode along with all those efforts to suppress, get rid, control, minimize, and neutralize obsessions.

The short story is that the more you try to control obsessions, the worse they get, and that's the essence of an OCD episode. I know you have been doing your best, and it makes total sense to try to get rid of something that's uncomfortable in the way that obsessions are, and yet, as far as I know, it's impossible to prevent obsessions from coming and going, up and down, left and right.

But, here is the big but, it's absolutely possible to learn to see obsessions for what they are—thoughts, images, urges that pop up in your mind—and not as dictators of your behavior.

The less you do those compulsions and avoidant or reassurance-seeking behaviors, the more you give yourself a chance to choose how to live your life! Kudos to you!

CHOOSING TO LIVE YOUR LIFE!

I'm so excited to introduce you to this section, because every time I explore and discuss these themes with my clients, it's the beginning of a rich, fun, and caring conversation and a new direction in our work together, an amazing one!

You know that dealing with OCD every day is like a full-time job without getting paid a good salary, and you may even forget that you can choose how to live your life and that you're the one in charge, not the obsessions that show up in your mind.

This section is all about helping you to choose how to be in this world, how to spend your time doing the things you care about, how to face your fears when it matters to you to do so, and how to practice your "choosing skills" to step forward into your life.

Choosing the life you want to live is a courageous step, and it doesn't happen automatically just by living one day to the next—there is no magic trick that makes it happen—it is really up to you to choose the life you want by taking every moment as an opportunity *to choose*.

No one is in a better position than *you* to choose how to move forward, and the truth is that taking actionable steps with patience, curiosity, and commitment will create the life you want to have.

Ready to practice your choosing skills? Give them a try!

CHAPTER 14

Choosing the Stuff You Care About!

Obsessions have so many ways of getting on your nerves, over and over, one after another, and as you recall from the previous chapter, the harder you try to manage them with avoidant, compulsive, or reassurance-seeking behaviors, the stronger they get—not to mention how time consuming it is to be living in a constant battle with obsessions. What if, instead of using all that effort, time, and resource trying to get rid of the obsessions problem or getting hooked on it, you actually focused on doing what truly matters to you? Imagine for a second how it would be to spend time doing all the things you care about.

When was the last time you thought about doing what you truly cared about doing? Some of my clients forget about it because they get so busy managing OCD episodes and getting distracted with all the noise that comes into their mind. Think for a moment about the trips you want to take, music you want to hear, games you want to play, or stuff you want to do with your friends. This section is all about helping you to learn all the ACT skills you need to know to handle those uncanny obsessions and disengage from compulsions and avoidant behaviors so that you can have more energy and time to have fun and do the things that really matter to you.

Let's start with a mini exercise.

Imagine for a moment that you wake up tomorrow and those uninvited obsessions were gone, completely gone. What would you do with your extra time? What would you want to do? And watch out when answering this question, because your obsessions will try to convince you that you can't do anything because of them—it's like they're a group of friends from high school that got together to complain and complain. But, while you hear them complaining, take a few moments to check the form below, and jot down what you would do differently in your life if this group of complainers weren't around.

If my uninvited obsessions are gone, I would…

At school	With friends
With my family	As a community member (think about different groups you may belong to: spiritual, sports, etc.)
With myself	

How did it go? Did you come to realize some of the things you care about? Or to confirm some of them you already knew were important to you?

And just to make sure we're on the same page, let me clarify that within ACT, when talking about the things that you care about, the stuff you care about, or the things that matter to you, they're called values. Imagine how it would be to live a life without doing the things we care about or living, just because…? Crazy, right?

Living your values is about checking in with yourself about what you want to stand for, what's important to you, and what you really want your life to be about. And to be clear, values are not the kinds of things that adults in your life want to choose for you or insist you should be doing. Identifying your values is really about you saying "I care about this..." and only you know what's deeply important to you deep down in your heart.

Below is a list of some examples of values that you can refer to as a guide for this chapter and moving forward. Keep in mind that this list is not exhaustive and it's just a guide. You might want to circle those that are important to you.

Saying what you think	Being accepting	Belonging
Being creative	Learning	Being real
Connecting	Being silly	Forgiving
Caring	Being humble	Knowing
Being healthy	Understanding others	Being open
Having freedom	Being curious	Discovering

You may have noticed that the stuff you care about is written with "action words" like being real, caring, understanding others, and so on. This is because within ACT we just don't talk about values, we put them into action as actions we choose to take day by day. For example, saying that one of my values is "love" sounds good, and it's a nice word, but it doesn't remind me that I can take steps every day to put that word into action. Saying "being loving" is different because it prompts me to put into action the behaviors that come along with "being loving" with the people I care about, and it also prompts me to keep in mind that living this value is not a one-time thing but an ongoing bunch of behaviors I choose to do. For example, being loving is not something I do just one time when talking to my sister, but a value that I choose to put into action in different relationships with people I care about and throughout my life. Do you see the difference?

Let's continue to discover what you truly care about. For this next exercise, think about a person you truly admire, respect, and are very fond of. This person can be someone in your family, a friend, a movie character, a sports person, a musician, a famous video-game player, etc. But think about a person you look up to and think about what qualities you admire in this person.

The person I'm a big fan of is:

_____

The qualities I appreciate in this person are:

_____

_____

_____

_____

_____

_____

Now take a look at your responses, and make a circle around those core qualities that person has that you would like to embrace for yourself. If you wrote many qualities, take another look and choose the ones that you really want to stand up for. For example, Nelson Mandela, a civil rights leader, chose to make his life about advocating against racial discrimination in South Africa. He was faced with a sentence of 27 years in prison and all that comes with losing your freedom in society, and yet, when asked about whether he would have done something different, he said he would do the same things over and over. Mandela was living his values, step by step and action by action.

TRY THIS!

And here is the last values-exploration activity for this chapter. Picture for a moment that you're celebrating your birthday at different times in your life, and people you care about and who matter to you are joining you in this celebration. You have managed to live your life in a way that truly matters to you. What would you want your friends and family to say about your personal qualities in a speech? As you image listening to them talk about your personal qualities, what do you hear them saying about you? Even if you're clear about what matters to you, I encourage you to go along with this exercise because you may discover new things!

When you turn 21	
When you turn 40	
When you turn 50	
When you turn 70	

Did you notice any similarities or differences in your response from the qualities you have already come to realize matter to you? Check whether there is a new quality that speaks to you from this last activity and make a circle around it.

Now, take a moment to review your responses in the three different values exercises you participated in, and jot down what you care about in the values-compass activity that follows:

At school: what type of student do you want to be?

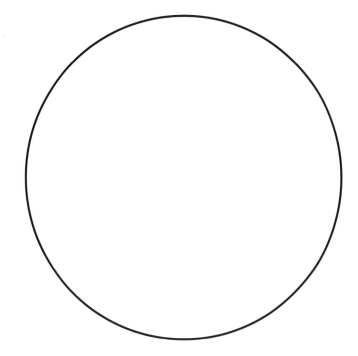

With my family: what type of relative do I want to be?

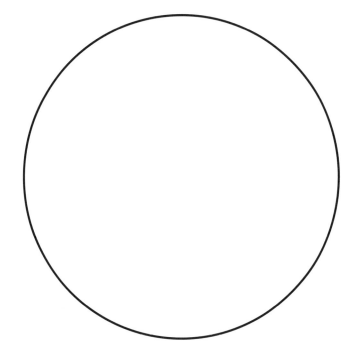

With friends: what type of friend do I want to be?

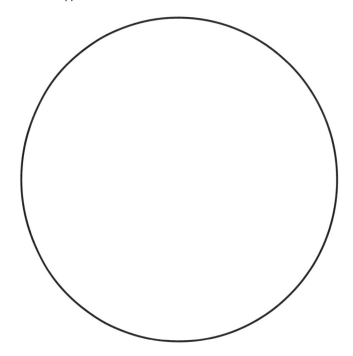

As a community member: what type of community member do I want to be? (Think about different groups you may belong to: spiritual, religious, sports, etc.)

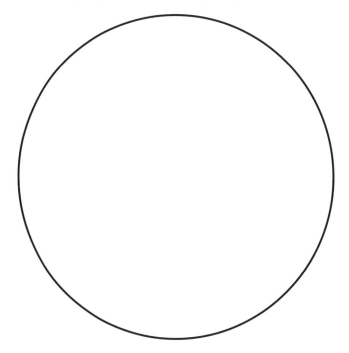

With myself: what type of person do I want to be? What type of relationship do I want to have with myself?

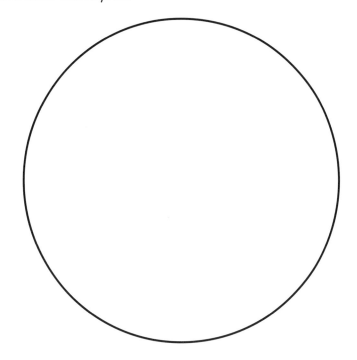

Kudos to you! You did an amazing job reviewing the stuff that matters to you. Learning to live your values is about imagining and dreaming about possibilities, even if you feel scared, fearful, and annoyed with the obsessions that make your dreams feel more challenging. Dealing with an obsession, as impossible as it can seem, does not have to block you from moving forward with your life. And in this workbook, you are learning specialized skills to do just that!

TRY THIS!

Using the Choice Point graphic below, jot down your values on the top right of it, above the words "Towards the stuff I care about," so you are clear about what matters to you. And hang in there. Little by little, you're learning different skills to handle those unsolicited obsessions and live life to the full.

For instance, after looking at my values as a daughter, my Choice Point looks like:

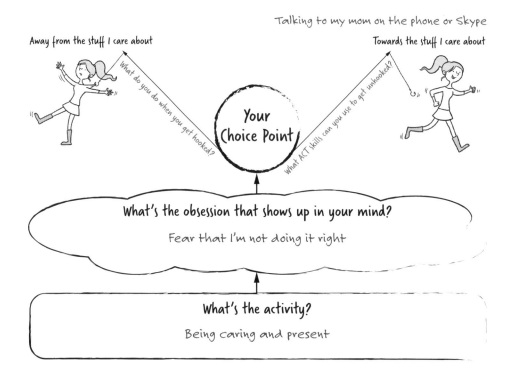

Now, go ahead!

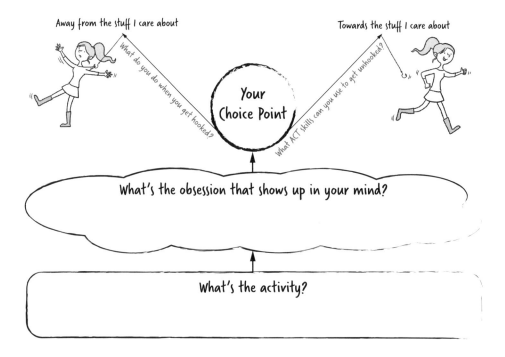

I truly hope that after completing this chapter you have more clarity about who you want to be and what type of person you want to be in different areas in your life so that you can invest all your time, energy, and resources into doing what truly matters to you.

Here's a quick tip for you before you move forward towards doing what matters to you: Living your values doesn't mean that you will not have uncanny thoughts, bizarre images, dragging impulses, fear, anxiety, or uneasiness. Living your values means that, as you've learned, the less you get hooked on your obsessions by trying to push them down, making visits to Compulsion City, wearing your fastest running shoes to get away from them, or asking for accommodations, the more time you'll spend living your life.

There is no one better than you to *choose* how to live your life!

CHAPTER 15

Doing the Stuff You Care About!

Years ago, when I was traveling from Bolivia to Brazil I decided to take a mini trip in the Amazon rainforest. It was a trip I had wanted to take for years and, finally, I had a chance to do it, so I was very excited. I prepared my hiking boots, carried light clothing, and took a book for the evenings. Every day of the tour we woke up around 6 a.m. and spent hours hiking and seeing all types of animals like small monkeys, parrots, wild pigs, crocodiles, and much more. Our guide knew the routes back and forth, so we never had to worry about finding our way back to our camp at the end of the day. The last day of this adventure, our regular tour guide couldn't come, so we got assigned a new one. This new guide seemed nice, friendly, and eager to show us the wilderness of the area. So, as usual, we started hiking for hours, taking pictures, and whispering sometimes to avoid scaring the animals. After having some light refreshments, we were ready to continue our hike, so we looked at the guide and asked which direction we should start walking in, but there was a problem: the guide wasn't sure which path to take. In an area where you're surrounded by such humongous trees that you cannot see the sky, that has very humid weather, and you're sweating and sweating, being confused or lost is a tough spot to be in. After maybe one hour of trying one path or another, and having all types of thoughts in my mind, the guide eventually figured out how to take us back to the camp and I was able to make it on time to take my plane that night.

This memory of feeling lost in the Amazon came to mind when writing this chapter about "doing what you care about," and with it, the acknowledgement that we all feel lost, confused, or scared in our life at different times. It's only when we pay attention to what deeply speaks to our heart, our values, that we find direction again. Your values are the best compass you have that will give you a sense of direction at every moment you're alive so that you can live your life as you choose to do so and handle your OCD episodes as they come.

Now, let's be realistic. You cannot live your life to the full by simply listing your values. You live your values by setting goals and taking specific steps towards them with your mouth, hands, and feet. You need to actually *do* the stuff you care about! And, to make it crystal clear, there is a difference between values and goals or actions: think about values as showing you the direction you want to go in, and goals and actions as the steps to take to move you towards your destination.

For example, John, who struggles with a fear of germs, cares deeply about protecting animals and his goal is to volunteer at the animal shelter one day a week. Marissa, who deals with obsessions about harming others, was actually very invested in "creating art." That was her personal value, so she spent every Saturday morning drawing a new object as an action towards the stuff she cares about.

Did you notice that John and Marissa's goals are behaviors that you can check off as done? That's a very important distinction: goals are your behaviors, or steps you take, whereas values are about whom you want to be and what you care about. Goals are usually going to answer the "wh" questions like when, what, with whom, and where to give you specific steps so you can check whether you accomplish them or not.

Let's do a mini exercise to practice this distinction between values and goals/actions:

For this exercise, match each description with either values and activities:

Values	Petting a dog
Values	Eating ice-cream with friends
Values	Being caring
Values	Having courage
Activity	Searching new music
Activity	Watching movies with my best friend
Activity	Helping others
Activity	Being trustworthy

Sometimes, when discussing with my clients their values, I hear things like "being respected" or "feeling loved," or other stuff related to others' behaviors, like "not letting my friend ignore me." Those are not personal values but wishful thoughts about others' behaviors. You can hope, expect, and wish to be treated in a particular way, but you don't have control of how other people behave or feel about you. If you find yourself stuck there, check again with yourself what's truly important to you.

Choosing and living the stuff you care about is not about getting rid of the fear, anxiety, or discomfort that comes along with your obsessions, because, as you have learned in this workbook, we don't have control of the stuff that the content generator of our minds comes up with. But, the important point is that you can start living your life while carrying with you those unwanted fears.

For the next activity, look back at the values-compass activity you completed in Chapter 14, "Choosing the Stuff You Care About!" and go over your responses. After reading your responses, here is what you need to do on the form below: For each one of those values areas—friendships, school, family, or community member—write down your values for each one of those areas and, in the next column, specific actions you would like to take towards your values.

ACTING ON THE STUFF YOU CARE ABOUT: VALUES-ACTION ROADMAP

Values in different areas of your life	What are the goals or actions you want to take to do the stuff you care about?
Friendships Example: connecting with others	Example: going to watch movies with Natalie once a month
School Example: learning about the world	Example: studying history only for 30 minutes three times a week
Community Example: being part of a group	Example: go to Mass twice a month
Family Example: collaborating	Example: do my weekend chores such as folding clothes and cleaning the living room
Self Example: being real	Example: saying what I think even though people may not like it.

Now that you have a sense of how you want to put into action the stuff you care about, make a note of this roadmap or bookmark it because this is going to be your roadmap for the next section when you learn unhooking skills to tackle those pesky obsessions while doing what matters to you with your feet!

TRY THIS!

Using the Choice Point graphic, jot down at the bottom of it one of the activities that you want to do because it really matters to you.

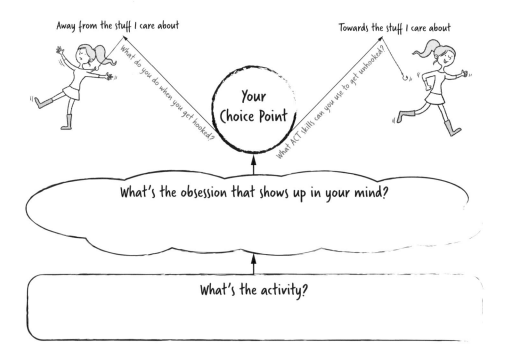

The Choice Point graphic may look quite simple right now, but it's just an illustration to highlight that, every single moment, you can actually choose how to live your life. I know you're busy and you have hundreds of things to do—studying, reading, playing soccer, eating ice-cream, taking a nap—but moving forward, you may want to check what things move you toward the stuff you truly care about and what stuff takes you away from it.

And, as I have said throughout this workbook, there is no one better than *you* to check what you're doing and why you're doing it, and there's no one better than you to know what price you pay in your life by going to Compulsion City and Escape City.

Remember that for the next section, "Getting Unhooked!," you're going to need to go back to your values-action roadmap many times. So again, you may want to make a mark on that page so you can easily go back to it!

CHAPTER 16

Checking Your "Fightonometer" When Doing Stuff You Care About

Choosing the stuff you care about is one thing, but doing the stuff you care about is a completely different thing. Often, that's one of the moments in which my clients get stuck—when it comes to actually putting into action what's really important to them. It's like when you're learning to speak Italian: you get to the point where you can understand, read, and write well enough, but then walking in the streets of Rome and actually speaking the language there is tricky because you may feel anxious, scared about making a fool of yourself, concerned you will blush, and worried about not being understood because you're afraid your accent is so bad. It's difficult, even though you really want to practice Italian because you value learning about other cultures.

When I chat with my clients about those sticky moments, I usually learn that they get stuck, not because they don't want to put into action what they care about, but because there is something else going on. What about trying a quick experiment to see how this goes for you? And keep in mind that there is no right or wrong way of doing this exercise. Just give it a try.

Grab a piece of paper and a pen and write down the name of one of your best friends. After writing down their name, next to it write down something bad happening to them. For example, I wrote this:

Annabelle died instantaneously in a car accident.

If you completed the experiment, what did you notice? If you didn't complete it, what reactions did you have?

If you're like one of the clients I work with, you may have noticed a bit of discomfort when completing this task, because, let's face it, who wants to write about something bad happening to one of your best friends? I certainly don't want it to happen, but having a thought about it and putting it on a piece of paper, or saying it aloud, is just putting letters, words, and sentences together. But of course, the content generator machine of our mind demands we take this sentence seriously and, on top of that, there is a bunch of feelings that come along with it: fear, guilt, sadness...or maybe a blend of them.

Do you go through a similar process when dealing with obsessions about contracting an illness, having a not-so-right feeling, an image about becoming a monster, or doubts about whether you curse at someone or not? Your mind over-focuses on those images, thoughts, sensations, or urges in the moment, and the emotions that come along with them can be so overwhelming that all of this together activates your fightonometer. Your fightonometer is all the efforts you make to push down or replace those fearful feelings, distract yourself, go into compulsion mode, or avoid whatever started those obsessions. But—here is the big but—that mini battle you go through with your obsessions and feelings just makes the struggle last longer. Turning on your fightonometer makes you feel stuck and takes away the time you could be spending doing the stuff you really care about. By now, you know that there is no winning when you try to control those feelings, even with the countless, and very creative, ways you have of trying to control them. And, needless to say, there is no winning when fighting the content generator machine of your mind, because it's like arguing with a brick wall.

Wherever you go, your feelings are going to show up, and there is no way around that. Putting into action what you care about is going to come with those sticky moments, but if you want to live life to its fullest, you may actually need to turn down the intensity of your fightonometer, drop your fight against those fears or urges that come along, and actually make room for them. You don't have to like, love, or cherish them, but just make space for them as they come.

Let's try another exercise:

Can you picture a walnut in your mind for a second? What would you say the walnut looks like? If I had to describe it, I would say something along the lines of a small brown fruit, circular or oval, covered with many wrinkles, of all sizes and widths. Would you agree with this description? If you're not sure, search online for the image of a walnut and use that image for the next exercise. Ready? Let's do this.

Get a timer, set it for 1 minute, and do your best to make a face like a walnut by squeezing and tensing every single area of your face—your eyes, mouth, and lips—against each other. And while making this walnut face, see if you can notice any tension in your facial expression around the eyes, nose, or mouth area. When the timer goes off, jot down below how it felt to make this walnut face:

_____

_____

_____

_____

Afterwards, set the timer again for 1 minute, make a walnut face again, but this time, just after squeezing your eyes, nose, and lips against each other as hard as you can, release all your facial muscles until the timer goes off. Jot down your reactions to this second exercise:

_____

_____

_____

_____

How did it feel to you to tense your face versus relaxing it? Did you notice the difference between holding your facial muscles tight, as if you're fighting against those squeezing sensations, and releasing them, as if you're turning down the volume of your fightonometer?

In your day-to-day life, perhaps you could choose—intentionally—to make room for those unwanted feelings, thoughts, memories, images, urges, and obsessions that come along, and to turn down the fightonometer in order to help you do the stuff you care about?

You may wonder, how do I turn down the fightonometer? Here are the basic steps that you can apply anywhere you are and at any time.

1. The first step is to *check when the fightonometer is turned on.*

     Usually your fightonometer is on when you cannot let those overwhelming feelings, obsessions, urges, or sensations go and you have a strong pull to do something about them right there, wherever you are. Another cue to check if your fightonometer is on is recognizing if you're judging what you're experiencing with words like "This is bad, wrong," and so on.

2. *Check and describe to yourself what you're feeling or thinking* by saying, "I'm having the [thought, urge, feeling] of _____."

3. *Check what's happening in your body.*

     For example, notice and describe to yourself your breathing, your heartbeat, your temperature, any areas of body tension. You could say, "My heart is beating fast, I notice my body is warm," and so on.

4. *Check what you feel like doing in that moment.*

5. *Check if, intentionally and actively, you can relax your body* by taking a deep breath, relaxing your muscles, or moving your body left to right a little bit.

6. *Choose in that moment what's important to you*: Is it worthwhile continuing to fight with those uncomfortable experiences? If not, check and describe to yourself your physical surroundings.

Turning down your fightonometer from all the inside noise that is happening under your skin will give you room to step back and choose your response. And if you follow these steps, I want to invite you to be curious to check how it goes for you. What you may be surprised to find out is that when you turn down your fightonometer and do nothing other than follow the above steps, the inside noise will follow its own course, like a wave. Sometimes it will be on the ascent—gathering strength; sometimes it will be at its peak; and sometimes—on the descent—it will be decreasing in intensity and strength.

But, if you continue to fight against it, then it's quite likely it will stay at the peak for quite a while and you may get stuck there.

Doing the stuff that we care about and taking actionable steps comes with inside noise—there is no way around it. For example, for me, writing this workbook comes with all types of feelings—like excitement, tiredness, frustration, fear, joy—and judgmental thoughts, such as "I'm not a good writer, what am I doing? No one is going to read this," and so on. And yet, because I care deeply about disseminating ACT for the specific struggles my clients are dealing with, I choose to sit and write on a regular basis while having all the inside noise come along every time I write. Of course, it's not easy-peasy because my fightonometer gets activated all the way up, but noticing the inside noise, naming it as "this is fear, this is anxiety, my heart is beating fast, I'm having a judgment thought," checking what truly matters to me, and then intentionally going back to paying attention to my writing keeps me going and also keeps me doing the stuff I care about. You can do it too! And I encourage you to do it too!

The more you work on this workbook, the better it's going to be, because every chapter will prompt you to check whether you are fighting the inside noise or letting it be when moving along your day. Just keep in mind that, no matter what, you can choose what you care about, and when doing what you care about, you need to check your fightonometer to see whether you're turning its volume up or turning it down!

TRY THIS!

You just finished learning about another core skill to get unhooked from your obsessions: checking your fightonometer! This week, if you have an OCD episode, reflect on it using the Choice Point graphic. Check whether your fightonometer was on or off. If it was on, then you know where it goes—yes, as a move away on the left side of the graphic—but, if you found yourself letting those obsessions and the fear, panic, and anxiety come and go as a wave, then that sounds like a move towards the stuff you care about.

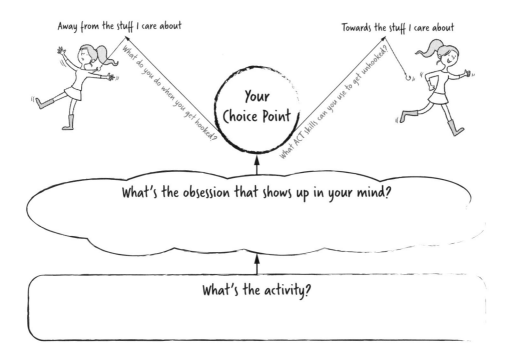

And now, it's time to learn and practice how to get unhooked from those annoying obsessions and *choose* to *do* what matters to you!

TAKEAWAYS!

Let's face it. What matters to you can get lost in the middle of an OCD episode, and yet, it's there within you.

In this section you figured out or confirmed the stuff you really care about in your life, identified specific actions to do what matters to you, and learned to check whether fighting against those overwhelming feelings, worries, anxieties, and stressful sensations takes you closer or further away from your personal values.

I'm really excited you finished this section on dreaming about the life you want to live, a life that is chosen by you and nobody else, and a life in which, no matter where you go, you will have all types of experiences: fun ones, tricky ones, and challenging ones. The more you distinguish what you have control of and what you don't, the more skillful you are going to get at living an amazing life!

Keep moving, keep living!

GETTING UNHOOKED!

Welcome to one of my favorite sections in this workbook: unhooking skills.

Quick question for you: Have you ever been at the top of a mountain from which you could see far into the distant landscape? If so, you know how it feels and what it looks like. This section is about exactly that: teaching you to look at your thoughts, images, memories, and all types of content that your mind comes up with from a distance!

You will learn specific skills to disengage, separate, and unhook from those pesky obsessions so you can stop being bossed around by them and focus on doing the stuff you care about!

Learning unhooking skills may be difficult in the beginning, as many new skills are, but it's completely worth it to put them into practice and use them to get your life back on track. Try them out, make them yours, and check which ones work for you. If you find yourself rushing through these chapters, slow down, give yourself time to play with the skills you are learning, and see how they work. You may want to consider trying one or two unhooking skills a week. If some of these unhooking skills don't work for you then, of course, don't use them. Do keep in mind that an unhooking skill *works*, not by making the obsession go away, but by having it as it is, and doing what's important to you.

You will have many unhooking skills to choose from—saying, singing, writing them down, hanging in there with obsessions, to name a few—and it's worth giving them all a try.

Be patient, practice over and over, and be patient again. Learning to hold those unsolicited obsessions lightly and living the stuff you care about is taking action every moment, step after step, and skill after skill!

Enjoy!

CHAPTER 17

Picturing and Naming Your Obsessions

Have you noticed how active your mind is?

Close your eyes for a minute and then listen to all the chitchat that shows up in the content generator of your mind. If you have thoughts like "I don't hear anything; there is nothing happening," that's your mind coming up with thoughts, right there! For me, for example, when I completed this exercise, my mind was thinking: "Do I like that song? What time is it? I like that yellow. What happened with my mom? Why is the heater not working?"

Did you notice the random thoughts my mind came up with? What about yours?

Even though your mind is already keeping an internal dialogue without you doing anything, when you are dealing with OCD this dialogue gets louder and louder, and all the more when you start doing more of the stuff you care about. OCD has a funny way of showing up and inundating you with obsessions that, if taken too seriously, can stop you from doing the stuff you care about for hours, days, and months.

Here is a great first skill to use to get unhooked from obsessions: picturing and giving your obsession a name! Yup, as silly as it sounds, picturing and naming is a very important skill because it will help you to recognize those obsessions when they pop up.

Here is how to put this skill into action: When one of your obsessions shows up, see if you can picture it in your mind with a particular shape, color, or texture, or the image of a cartoon, or even as a fictitious character, or any other image you come up with. Then name it based on this image!

For example, Chris, who struggles with the "fear of forgetting important things" and spends hours and hours compulsively writing down the conversations he has with people he cares about, named his obsession "Mr. Octopus" because, in Chris's opinion, his obsession clutches onto every single conversation he has. He pictures this octopus as purple, medium size, and holding notes of a conversation in every tentacle.

Here is another example: Anna gets inundated with obsessions about "harming the environment," so at school she makes sure to pick up all the scrap paper her classmates leave on their desks, and all the garbage she finds on the patio during recess. At church, she collects all the plastic caps, and at home, she really struggles using paper plates when her parents have a large party. Anna is so concerned about harm to the environment that she can't sleep, misses playing with her friends during recess, and dreads every party either held at home or that she is invited to because of all the trash there will be to collect. When Anna was mapping her OCD episodes using the exercises from Section 3, "Meeting the 'Annoying Obsessions,'" she noticed her obsession showed up as an image of "the earth covered in plastic." Anna decided to name her obsession "Ronna, the cleaning lady" and pictured her as a perky little lady, wearing an apron, carrying a broom and a shovel, wearing special boots to go into all types of soil, and a bit wiped out from cleaning all the time.

You can give your obsessions all types of names and picture them in as many forms as you please. There are no rules, and it's all up to your imagination! Over the years working as a therapist, I have heard names like: Mr. Clean; the return of the gremlin; I'm trapped thoughts; Ms. forecaster imperfecta; hooking thoughts; and so on. There are really no limits to your imagination when it comes to naming and picturing those obsessions. You can also just call them "my obsessions" and imagine what they look like. It's really up to you to choose what works best!

Picturing and naming your obsessions will help you to distinguish them from other thoughts that show up in your mind so that you can choose your response to them, which is very different from automatically doing what those pesky obsessions push you to do. Picturing and naming obsessions is the first step to practice your super-choosing skills!

TRY THIS!

It's your turn to picture and give a name to your obsessions! In the next form, jot down your obsessions and next to each of them draw what the obsession looks like and give it a name. Do your best to add a personal touch!

What is the unsolicited obsession that your mind is coming up with?	Give the obsession a name, picture how it looks, and draw it here.
What is the unsolicited obsession that your mind is coming up with?	Give the obsession a name, picture how it looks, and draw it here.
What is the unsolicited obsession that your mind is coming up with?	Give the obsession a name, picture how it looks, and draw it here.
What is the unsolicited obsession that your mind is coming up with?	Give the obsession a name, picture how it looks, and draw it here.

How was it for you looking at the names and images you came up with for your obsessions? The more you practice this unhooking skill, the better you're going to get at catching those pesky obsessions before they catch *you*!

UNHOOK!

In every chapter of this section, you're going to find an "unhooking practice" segment dedicated to put into action the values-action roadmap you came up with in Chapter 15, "Doing the Stuff You Care About!" So, every week you will be using the Choice Point graphic to prepare for taking a step towards your values, and then putting it into action!

While you're prompted to use the Choice Point graphic once a week, at the bare minimum, in every chapter, I really want to encourage you, if poss-ible, to do it more than once a week to continue practicing unhooking skills.

Here are the steps for you to complete the Choice Point graphic:

1. Choose an area you care about, like school, family, friendships, or community.

2. Choose a specific activity you want to do, and make sure to specify when, with whom, what time, and for how long you want to do it. It's really up to you to choose what activity you want to do, and it's okay to choose a small activity. As long as you choose something, that's what matters moving forward. Do you remember that in Chapter 15, "Doing the Stuff You Care About!," you were asked to make a note of the values-action roadmap? If you want, you can take a peek at it and use it as guidance for this part.

3. Write down the unwanted obsession that shows up in the thought-bubble.

4. Under the area "Away from the stuff I care about," jot down all the compulsions, avoidance, or requests for accommodations you usually do that keep you hooked on your obsessions.

5. Under the area "Towards the stuff I care about," you will usually jot down all the unhooking skills you could use and will learn in this section and the rest of the workbook. In this chapter in particular, you learned an unhooking skill, picturing and naming, and, if you recall, in Section 5, "Choosing to Live Your Life!," you learned the skill of turning down your fightonometer, so you can hang in there with the uneasiness, fear, jumpiness, and anxiety that come along with bothersome obsessions.

Don't worry if, right now, you don't know many unhooking skills to write down. You just started learning about them, and as you move along in this workbook, every chapter is going to introduce a new unhooking skill for you to try out!

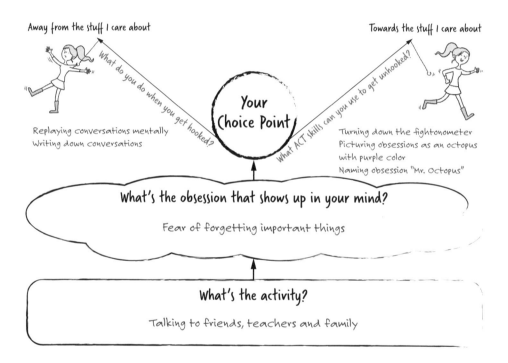

Away from the stuff I care about

Towards the stuff I care about

What do you do when you get hooked?

What ACT skills can you use to get unhooked?

Your Choice Point

Replaying conversations mentally
Writing down conversations

Turning down the fightonometer
Picturing obsessions as an octopus with purple color
Naming obsession "Mr. Octopus"

What's the obsession that shows up in your mind?

Fear of forgetting important things

What's the activity?

Talking to friends, teachers and family

Your turn to complete your Choice Point!

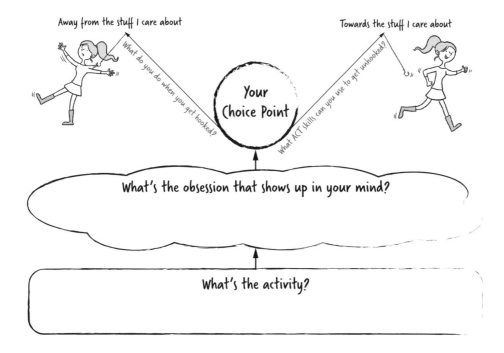

Now you can see what the Choice Point graphic looks like as a whole when you complete all parts of it. Really handy, right?

Go back to the values-action roadmap from Chapter 15, "Doing the Stuff You Care About!," and use it as guidance for putting into action steps towards a particular value of yours every day. If you're already doing the stuff you care about, maybe you want to try a new behavior. After choosing a value and a respective action for it, use the Choice Point graphic to prepare for it, and catch those regular behaviors that keep you hooked, as you did in the activity above. Ideally, complete your Choice Point graphic every day, but if you can't, start with once a week! Every effort matters!

Don't forget, you can find a blank Choice Point graphic in Appendix 1 or download and print copies from www.jkp.com/catalogue/book/9781787750838.

TIP FOR THE WEEK

At the end of every chapter in this section, you're going to read quick recommendations to practice a skill (in addition to completing your Choice Point graphic) or some advice I may have for you for this week.

And to start, here is your tip for this week: If at any point in your day, the content generator machine comes up with those obsessions unexpectedly, do your best to picture them in your mind and give them a name! The more you do it, the more you will get unhooked and make moves towards what you care about!

CHAPTER 18

Watching Your Obsessions in Front of You

This chapter is going to show you how to use your imagination to "watch your obsessions" as you watch hundreds of other things day by day. Those unwelcome obsessions, as annoying as they are, are simply made up of words and images that are popping up in your mind all the time. They only take power from you when you get hooked on them by trying to replace them with a different thought, arguing against them with logic, doing a compulsion, or getting out of a triggering situation as soon as possible.

First, a couple of questions to introduce you to this unhooking skill: How often do you go to the library or to a book store? How often do you check your email account? It's likely you have done either or both of those activities, many times, so you know that when you go to the library and look at the shelves, you see many books with titles without opening them. You also know that when you check your email, you see the subject of an email without opening it.

Imagine your uninvited obsessions in front of you, as if you're just watching them, without opening them up or checking their content.

For example, Ryan loved listening to music and wanted to see his favorite band in a concert, but he was very worried about having to go into the city by train and about being around his friends without knowing whether they had washed their hands or not. Ryan was concerned about them touching him, getting germs, and getting sick for an undefined period of time.

Using the skill of picturing the obsession and giving it a name, Ryan named his obsession "Mr. Protector," and imagined it as a superhero with a big black cap. Ryan also noticed that when "Mr. Protector" came into action, it shouted all types of things, like "You don't know what they have touched, what if you get sick? What if they have germs?" Using this new unhooking skill, Ryan was able to imagine those thoughts as they were coming from Mr. Protector. He pictured Mr. Protector shouting out all kinds of warnings in the same way as could look at the titles of the books he never opened or songs listed in iTunes he didn't care to listen to.

You could also imagine and watch those obsessions in front of you as:

- the subject of the email in the inbox

- labels of your favorite cereal

- names of dishes on a menu

- names of countries

- printed letters on a t-shirt

- apps in your cellphone

- emojis.

What other suggestion would you add to the above list? Any other way to imagine and observe those obsessions in front of you? If so, write them below:

_____

_____

_____

_____

A client of mine, who liked fantasy movies, imagined his obsessions as orbs and came up with the following drawing:

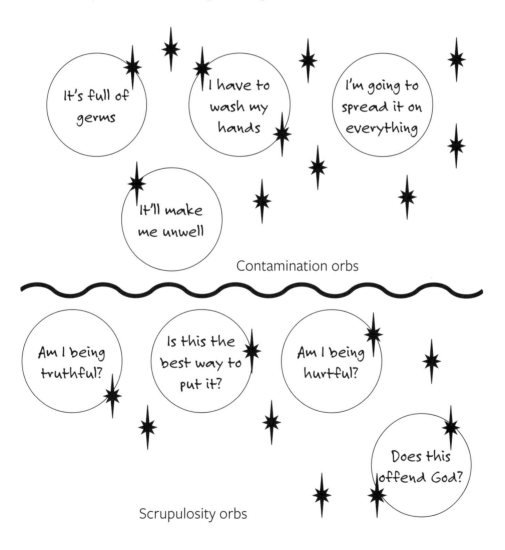

It's full of germs

I have to wash my hands

I'm going to spread it on everything

It'll make me unwell

Contamination orbs

Am I being truthful?

Is this the best way to put it?

Am I being hurtful?

Does this offend God?

Scrupulosity orbs

TRY THIS!

Now, give it a try:

Choose any of the suggested images in the section above or any other idea you come up with to imagine watching the obsessions that the content generator of your mind shouts at you. Jot it down! Go for it and have fun using your imagination!

UNHOOK!

Using the Choice Point graphic over and over is going to help you to visualize the Choice Point graphic in your head so you can remember that you can choose to unhook from those obsessions as you go about your day-to-day life!

If you're unsure how to complete the Choice Point graphic, take a peek at the "unhooking practice" segment from the last chapter (Chapter 17), "Picturing and Naming Your Obsessions," and follow the same steps 1–5. Of course, feel free to choose a different value or a different action you want to focus on for this week.

Preparing a values-based behavior with the Choice Point graphic is one thing. The next is for you to actually do it! Ultimately, this workbook is about practicing and practicing until it becomes natural for you to use the Choice Point in your day-to-day life!

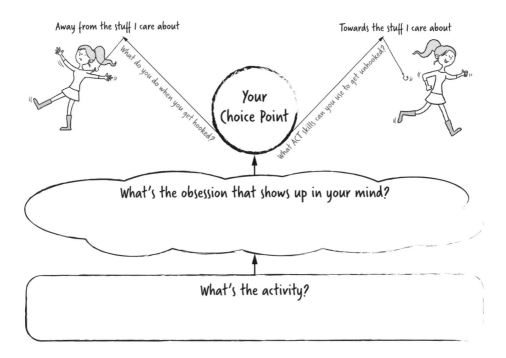

TIP FOR THE WEEK

Moving forward, every time you catch your obsessions showing up in the middle of whatever you're doing, put into practice this skill: imagine that obsession and watch it as something to observe, appreciate, notice, and simply watch again, rather than something to fight against. You can try a different image every time the obsession pops up and see how it goes for you.

Learning to watch your thoughts won't make the obsessions go away, but will help you to get unhooked so you can focus your energy on the stuff you care about!

Now that you have practiced watching your obsessions, let's take this skill one step further: putting your obsessions into action!

CHAPTER 19

Putting Your Obsessions into Action!

Do you like to watch movies by any chance? I personally absolutely love to watch movies of all types, except horror movies. But what comes to my mind about movies when writing this chapter is this: When a film is being shot, someone shouts "Scene 1, action" and then the actors start performing, doing anything from portraying someone in a sad scene, to singing, fighting, etc.

In this chapter, you're going to be like a director of the movie of your obsessions and put them into action! In the end, obsessions can be like actors that will follow your lead!

Why not try directing your obsessions by picturing them as one of the following?

- Actors on stage that you, as a director, direct and watch from the audience

- Soccer players with t-shirts that have the obsessions printed on them and you're watching them running in the field

- Ad banners on taxi cabs passing by that you watch from the street

- Guests dancing all over the floor

- Planes flying banners with obsessions that you can see moving in the sky.

For instance, Janine always carried a hand sanitizer in her backpack and reached to it as a compulsion every time she thought she touched something that may have had germs on it, like books or papers that were handed to her in class or at the library. Using this unhooking skill, Janine imagined her obsessions as clouds moving in the sky and each one of them had messages like "This is not clean enough. Who touched this? Did this person wash his hands before touching it? What if he didn't? How many people have used this book before?"

TRY THIS!

See if you can come up with any other image for these obsessions that shows them moving, up and down, left and right, or use any of the suggested images above.

Draw the obsessions-into-action here

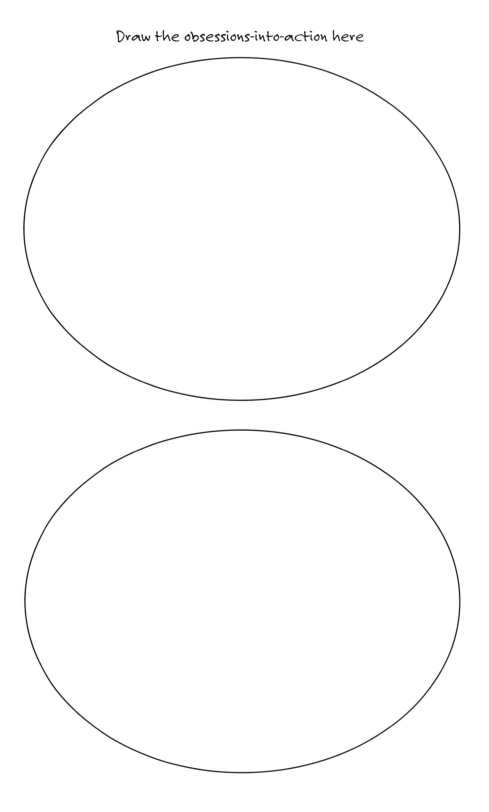

UNHOOK!

Ready to make a bold move towards your values this week? Did you take a peek at your values-action roadmap? If the answer is yes to both of these questions, yay! Go ahead, jump into your Choice Point, use it to organize doing the stuff you care about, anticipate potential hooks—asking for accommodations, avoidance, and compulsions—and list the unhooking skills you could use to handle that sticky moment of choice!

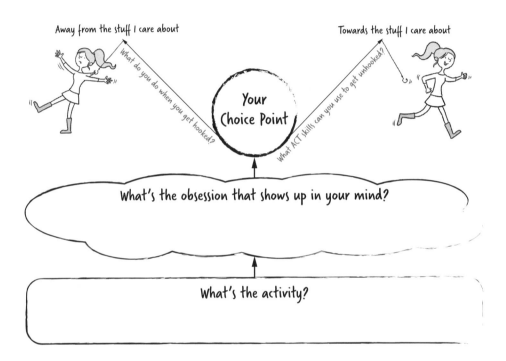

TIP FOR THE WEEK

A mini reminder for you: You cannot stop your obsessions from popping up in your mind, but you don't have to get hooked on them every time they show up. You can choose stuff you care about, do stuff you care about, turn down your fightonometer, and use unhooking skills when the unsolicited obsessions show up.

CHAPTER 20

Saying Your Obsessions

Our minds keep on moving wherever we go. Non-stop, 24/7, there are no holidays or vacations for the content generator machine of our mind! It comes up with all types of thoughts over and over.

Some of those thoughts are very handy for what you want to do, like the image of that chemistry formula that you need to remember when taking a chemistry test, or a thought about the upcoming office hours you have with your math teacher.

However, when dealing with OCD episodes, you're bombarded with all sorts of fearful thoughts—fears about cursing at others, physically attacking people you care about, committing immoral acts, cursing things that you usually won't say, or harming yourself—that come with a strong sense of urgency, as if you have to take action right away. By now, you know that that's what obsessions try to do: they push you to do something, to run away, and to reduce the fear, anxiety, and worry that comes along with them as quick as possible. For example, Brandon battles with an obsession of "becoming a bad character in a movie," so when having this thought, he compulsively, and at the speed of light, imagines he's covering his eyes with his hand just to make sure he doesn't become the character of that particular movie.

Your mind keeps moving and moving. There is not much you or I can do about it, but you can learn to hang in there with those obsessions, take a deep breath, and practice your response to having them. By now you know that having those obsessions means having a bunch of letters and words your overworking brain puts together, and as tough as they are, they are not what keeps OCD going—it's the compulsions or escaping behaviors that feed the OCD cycle.

So, let me introduce you to another handy skill in handling those pesky obsessions when they show up: saying to yourself that those obsessions are here!

Yup, you read it correctly. It may sound odd and even silly, but by simply saying to yourself that you notice the obsession and then naming it, you're calmly acknowledging it so that you can practice unhooking from it.

Below is what this skill looks like.

When catching yourself having one of those obsessions, instead of responding to the obsession, fighting against it, questioning it, or getting hooked on it, you can say things like:

"I'm having the obsessions of..."

"I notice I'm having the obsession of..."

"I'm spotting the obsession of..."

"I'm catching the obsession of..."

As an extension of this unhooking skill, you can also *notice the theme* of what your mind is doing and just say to yourself: "doubting, overthinking, thinking, worrying," etc.

TRY THIS!

Let's put this into practice.

Choose one or two obsessions you're dealing with and then write down any of the sayings you prefer.

Obsession you're dealing with: fear of stealing items from my classmates

Saying it: I'm spotting the fear of stealing items from my classmates

Your turn:

Obsession you're dealing with:

_____

Saying it:

_____

Obsession you're dealing with:

_____

Saying it:

_____

Saying the obsession doesn't make the obsession go away, but it does help you to step back and practice having those obsessions as stuff you have and not as stuff you fight, argue back with, respond to, or try to prove wrong!

UNHOOK!

Let's put into action the unhooking skill you learned in this chapter by completing your weekly Choice Point graphic so you can move towards the stuff you really care about instead of doing what the obsessions tell you to do. As you have been doing in every chapter of this section, make use of the Choice Point graphic to prepare yourself to do the stuff you care about! And after preparing for your values-based move using the Choice Point graphic, do it in real life, and see how it goes!

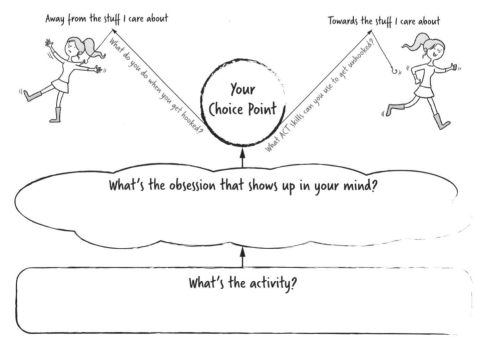

TIP FOR THE WEEK

Here is my recommendation for you for this week: Every time one of those obsessions shows up, practice noticing it, saying it using any of the words you read in this chapter, and see with a pinch of curiosity what happens!

And as you know, your priority is to complete your Choice Point, preferably every day! These tips are just that, tips for you to keep in mind.

CHAPTER 21

Singing Your Obsessions

Is there a singer or singers that you love and don't get tired of listening to their songs over and over? And if you're not that into music, is there any singer you like just a bit? Believe it or not, I have more than one favorite singer because I absolutely love music, but if I have to choose a singer that I like right now, as I write this chapter, I would say: Enanitos Verdes. Quite likely you haven't heard of them, they're a very old Latin band from the 70s, a looooooong time ago. They were as famous in South America as the Beatles were in the rest of the world. And I love their song "Lamento boliviano," which translates into English as "Bolivian lament." Despite this title, it's a song about accepting reality as it is, as it comes, as it is, and choosing to live and love. It seems to be that it's similar to the shift you're making right now: learning to accept what's outside of you and what's inside of you—especially when your mind comes up with all types of noise—and choosing to continue living your life!

Let's go over an unhooking skill that is a bit more adventurous, and it can be very handy when dealing with uncanny obsessions, bizarre images, or wild urges that float in your mind: singing your obsessions.

One time, when working with a client of mine dealing with fears about not doing things perfectly when completing schoolwork and spending hours checking and re-checking all his responses until it felt right, he decided to sing his obsessions to the tune of "No tears left to cry" by Ariana Grande. In session, we replaced some of the lyrics to be about his obsessions. Here is how it looked:

I'm feeling unprepared
I think I need to study more
I don't know the material
And it's not good enough, not good enough
Thinking and thinking
It's not good enough
It's not good enough
Not good enough

I'm thinking and thinking
It's not good enough
Thinking it up, thinking it up
I'm thinking and thinking
It's not good enough
Yeah, it's good enough

I need to study more
It's just a thought I like it
I think it, I think it
No matter how, where I try it,
It's in my mind yeah, my mind yeah

If you play the song by Ariana Grande, you will hear how these new lyrics go nicely with the tune. This is not about whether you can sing well or not, but to learn to say those obsessions aloud in different ways so they don't hijack you and take you away from what's truly important to you.

TRY THIS!

Your turn. To try out this unhooking skill you need a device to play one of your favorite songs. Listen to it, check the lyrics, write your own lyrics that involve your obsessions, and then sing your own lyrics to the tune of it. And please know that when I introduce this unhooking skill to my clients, we listen to the song they choose multiple times, and go back and forth with lyrics, until we get them.

Or, you can start with an easy and popular tune, the classic happy birthday song or a holiday song. Then you can try with your favorite song!

Psssst, if your mind is shouting at you, "It will be bad, I don't know how to sing," how about practicing one of the unhooking skills you have learned so far: picturing and naming, watching those thoughts in front of you, putting those thoughts into action, saying those thoughts?

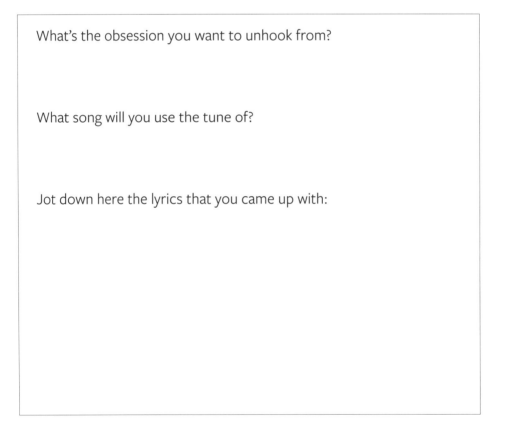

What's the obsession you want to unhook from?

What song will you use the tune of?

Jot down here the lyrics that you came up with:

After completing this, write down any reactions you had when practicing this unhooking skill:

_____

_____

_____

_____

UNHOOK!

No unhooking skill in this workbook can be developed without being applied to your day-to-day life! I encourage you to continue to go back to the wonderful values-action roadmap you came up with in Chapter 15, "Doing the Stuff You Care About!," and keep on using the Choice Point to plan a values-based activity one day a week. If you do it more than once, that's great!

   Go for it!

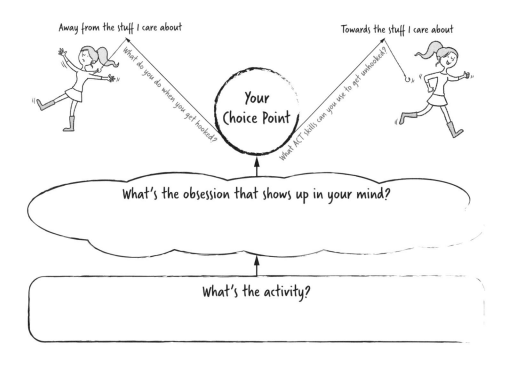

TIP FOR THE WEEK

As with any skill, the benefits come from trying it out over and over, and over and over again. And by benefits, I don't mean eliminating all your obsessions forever, but learning to live with them as a string of words, images, and memories that float through your mind. And the advantage of using these unhooking skills is that you don't need anything else besides openness to trying them out anytime, anywhere. There may be times when it's difficult. If so, give yourself a break, and when you're up for it, try it again!

CHAPTER 22

Writing Down Your Obsessions

Here is another one of my favorite unhooking skills: writing those obsessions down!

Remember that obsessions, as powerful and bossy as they seem, are simply letters and vowels that when put together form words and then sentences. But on their own they're powerless creations of your mind. It's only when you do what they say that those obsessive thoughts get power over you.

Let's begin. I know you do a lot of writing for school and quite likely you use a lot of pens and pencils. Now you are going to need a bunch of them for this unhooking skill.

First, write down those obsessions one by one on a piece of paper. Next, write them down again as Word Art! Imagine how pretty and neat those words would look as Word Art! If you're not into Word Art, you can write your obsessions with different types of font—cursive, bold, or italic and with different types of case—lower case, capital case, or a mixture of them. And if you're adventurous, you can use any Word Art application from the internet—they're pretty easy to use.

When Brian completed this exercise, his written obsessions looked like this:

If you want to take this unhooking skill a step further, what about writing a rhyme, a story, a poem, a rap song, or graffiti about this unwanted obsession?

TRY THIS!

As with everything you have been doing in this workbook, it's all about trying it out yourself!

Write down below the obsession you want to work on:

_____

_____

Using the shapes below, write down the same obsession in four different ways: different font, different color if you have pencil colors, different directions, and so on. Write it down in any style—there are no limits!

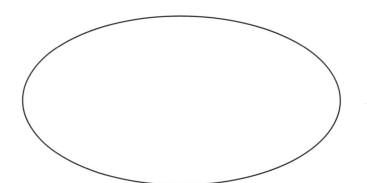

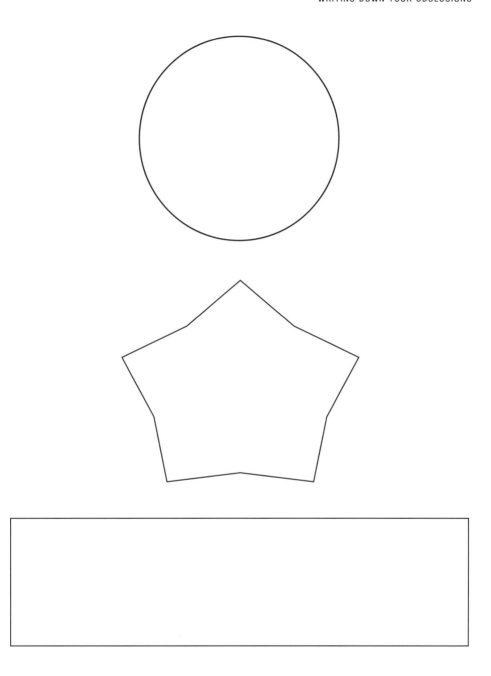

And lastly, imagine that you're a full-time writer and you have been asked to write a narrative about a particular obsession. What would that look like? See if you can jot down a story, a poem, or a news article about this uncanny thought. Of course, if you want, you can compose a song for it too!

[blank box]

On the lines below, write down any discoveries you had when completing these unhooking exercises:

_____

_____

_____

_____

_____

UNHOOK!

Have you noticed how you're taking steps toward the stuff that matters to you little by little?

Living and doing what matters is not easy, and of course, our mind, our content generator machine, makes all types of comments about it. But remember that we live our values with our feet, hands, and mouth. So whatever the size of an action you take—whether it is large, medium, small, or tiny—as long as you choose to take one, and not listen to the obsessions, you're making bold moves!

What about if, for this week, you choose three values-based activities, prepare for them, put them into action, and check how they go? Deal? Your call, of course!

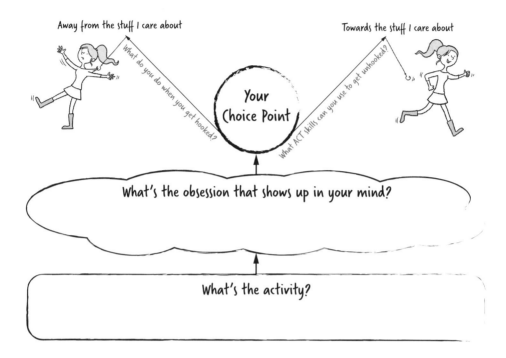

TIP FOR THE WEEK

Unhooking from your obsessions means separating from them, having them, seeing them for what they are, and allowing them to be as they are without trying to change, replace, or get rid of them.

By now, you have learned six different unhooking skills that you can play with when moving throughout your day and having distressing obsessions. With a pinch of curiosity, try any of them, and see what happens.

And before moving on, here is a big reminder for you of the goal and purpose of unhooking skills: using unhooking skills is not about getting rid of the obsessions but about practicing accepting them as they are, having them, hanging in there, and making room for them.

CHAPTER 23

Teasing Your Obsessions

Do you know how it feels to have a good laugh, to smile, or to be silly at times? What about making fun of your obsessions? Are you open to giving this unhooking skill a try?

Here is the main idea: When unsolicited obsessions float into your mind, you don't argue back with them or try to prove they're wrong, you just tease them, in the way that you may have teased your siblings, friends, parents, etc. You could exaggerate the things they are saying or repeat what they are saying in a silly voice. For example, Susan, a 14-year-old, had an obsessive fear that bad things would happen to her and her family if she didn't check the water faucet of all the bathrooms in the house and the kitchen. So she checked them all four times before going to sleep, and every time she was leaving the house, even when going to the backdoor patio. Susan started to repeat the things her obsession was saying in a high-pitched voice: "Silly me, I need to check the water faucets in the whole house, sure, one by one, I should do it 25 times, and not just 4." When she listened to herself saying those words aloud, it sounded so silly she started to laugh.

You can repeat what the obsession is saying in silly voices. For example:

- a favorite character from a video game

- a movie character

- a peculiar accent.

You can even use apps like Voice Changer to listen to your intrusive obsessions with different voices. You can give the obsession a silly scientific name and say things that rhyme with it (e.g. agressi-phur, baccilus, obsessivilus). And you can try to say your obsession in a different language, even if you don't fully speak that language.

Remember that unhooking is all about having those annoying obsessions without doing anything they tell you to do, even though they push you, full force, to do a compulsion, to avoid, or to ask for an accommodation. Imagine that your obsessions are like a puppy that follows you around begging for a treat, looking at you, doing cute tricks, and even staring at you. Do you give him a treat every time? Unless you want the puppy to get sick, you know you cannot do that. You keep doing what you're doing while the dog does its own things. Unhooking from obsessions is like that, it's letting those obsessions be without you taking any action.

TRY THIS!

As with everything you have been doing in this workbook so far, it's all about trying it out yourself!

Write down below the obsession you want to unhook from:

_____

_____

Choose a teasing unhooking skill and make a circle around it:

Character voices   Foreign language

Jot down what you could say for this unhooking skill:

_____

_____

_____

_____

And go!

Write down below any reactions you had when completing these unhooking exercises:

_____

_____

_____

_____

UNHOOK!

As you have been doing in every chapter in this section, it's time to put this new unhooking skill into action, plan for a values-based behavior, and make it happen in your day-to-day living! And again, I encourage you to choose one values-based activity a week, but as you progress, see if you can make it more often, like two or three times a week.

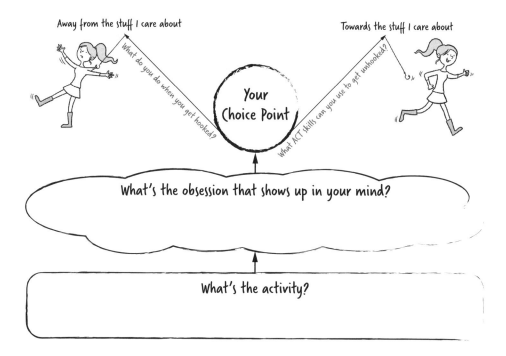

TIP FOR THE WEEK

Thoughts, all types of them, including annoying obsessions and ridiculous images, are going to come up in your mind again and again. You know that some of these thoughts are very important, like the stuff you have to do for school, planning a gathering with your friends, etc. Other thoughts are of no value at all to you, and yet there they are showing up again and again without any purpose.

Let me remind you, the more that you accept that having a mind means having a content generator machine that constantly comes up with all types of thoughts, the less you will fight against it and the better you're going to get at unhooking and moving along with your life. This week, in addition to putting your Choice Point into action with a values-based action, do your best to turn down your fightonometer when the fear, anxieties, worries, or panicky sensations come your way. Here are six quick steps for you to do when you notice any of the overwhelming emotions that come along with obsessions. I call them the 6Cs (each step starts with the letter "C"):

1. **C**heck if your fightonometer is on by recognizing what you're telling yourself: these feelings, thoughts, and urges are "bad, wrong, or a problem."
2. **C**heck and describe to yourself what you're feeling or thinking or sensing by saying, "I'm having the obsession, thought, urge, image, feeling of..."
3. **C**heck and describe to yourself what's happening in your body. For example, notice your breathing, your heartbeat, any areas of stress or discomfort.
4. **C**heck what you're driven to do in the moment—what do you feel like doing?
5. **C**heck if you can relax your body and take a deep breath.
6. **C**hoose in that moment what's important to you: is it worth continuing to fight with those uncomfortable experiences? If not, check and describe to yourself your physical surroundings.

Emotions, including fear, panic, anxiety, and worry, have a limited life—they have a beginning, a middle, and an end.

CHAPTER 24

Scrambling Up Your Obsessions

When I moved from Bolivia to the United States in 2001, I discovered what would become one of my favorite games: word scramble. First, I spent hours playing it with a dictionary next to me, then I started playing with my friends in Bolivia using the word scramble app. I was still using a dictionary—because English is my second language—and enjoying the game, but little by little, I was able to play every round without a dictionary.

Here is what I like about word scrambles: the many possibilities you have to combine multiple letters to put together an actual word and how careful you have to be when selecting the one that fits the bill the most. And, to be honest, at times it looks like you're just making a thought scramble.

For example, look at this word:

Y E I N T X A

What do the letters above spell? Did you get it? It spells "anxiety." I just took letters from the word, reorganized them, and there you have it—a new word based on those letters—but without the feeling associated with it because it's just a bunch of letters put together.

And if you look again, the word "anxiety" is just a word made up of letters that by itself doesn't need to mean anything, but the content generator machine generalizes its use to all situations, whether it helps you to move toward the stuff you care about or not. It's like when your mind notices the experience of fear, worry, panic, and anxiety in your body. It quickly pushes you to take it seriously—as something that has to be fixed, solved, and repaired immediately—even though there is really nothing to be solved and the best thing to do is to let that emotion run its own course.

And naturally, when you're dealing with an unwelcome obsession that comes along with fear, panic, or anxiety, your mind pushes you to act, to do something about it, to minimize, neutralize, decrease, and reduce the discomfort that comes with it. But, if you learn to have those obsessions as a bunch of letters and words that come along together, their power over you shifts, because you also learn to see them as a group of vowels and consonants that shows up in your mind—and just because they show up, that doesn't mean that they're the absolute truth. Obsessions can be so arrogant, don't you think?

This chapter will teach you how to make a thought scramble with your obsessions so they don't paralyze you with fear in your day-to-day living. Let's start making a thought scramble!

TRY THIS!

Write down the three most common obsessions you struggled with last month:

1. _____

2. _____

3. _____

Now, can you rewrite them in a different order?

For example, Ed had the obsession:

"What if I hit pedestrians and don't even know because I'm not careful enough?"

Then, when he scrambled these words, he came up with the following:

"If not pedestrians and I don't careful if enough because hit I'm even what."

Your turn:

1. _____

2. _____

3. _____

What did you notice when scrambling up your obsessions? The more you practice mixing up the words from your obsessions, the more I invite you to be curious about how it feels to repeat those words and what happens to the meaning that comes along with them. Is it the same as the original sentence? What changed?

And just to practice scrambling a thought one more time, take a peek at the activity below. Mary Oliver, an American poet, wrote the poem "Summer Day," but it looks like some of the words have been scrambled from the last part of this poem! Unscramble the words between the brackets to read the lines and write them down where they correspond!

Tell _____ [em]

What is it _____ [oyu]

_____ [nlap] to do

With _____ [uryo] one wild and _____ [uopsicre] life?

You know that no matter where you go, your mind can't help it, and will continue to come up with hundreds of thoughts, obsessions, images, memories, doubts, and hypotheses. No matter what, your mind will continue thinking and thinking. But instead of taking every thought, and in particular obsessions, as little bosses of your behavior, you can see that thoughts are made up of letters, they're not real things, or even your enemies. Thoughts are just thoughts.

UNHOOK!

By now, you know how to use the Choice Point graphic! What will you use it for this week?

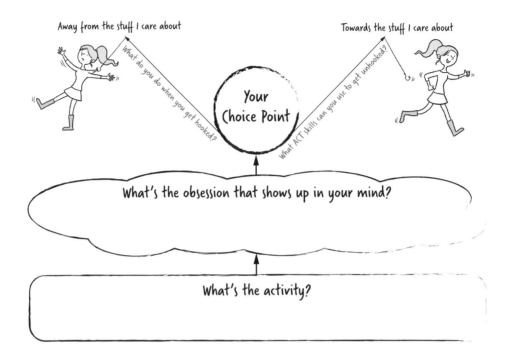

TIP FOR THE WEEK

Moving on with your day-to-day life, next time your mind comes up with an obsession, scramble it up, say it to yourself, and so on. Keep in mind that this unhooking skill is not about making the obsession go away but helping you to focus and refocus on what's happening in that particular moment of your day.

CHAPTER 25

Refocusing Your Attention

In this section you have learned many unhooking skills—from silly ones to those that use your creativity—that will help you practice having those annoying obsessive thoughts without acting on them. Kudos to you! I urge you to keep up with your practice every day, and at every triggering moment!

In this chapter, I would like to introduce you to a handy skill for handling those moments in which it's hard to let go of the obsessions and you're almost crushed with fear and close to giving in to compulsive behaviors: refocusing your attention. We can also call this skill grounding, or regrouping, as my clients call it. I know it's really hard not to engage in compulsions—otherwise, you wouldn't be using this workbook, right?

As you recall from Chapter 13, "Checking the Costs of Getting Hooked," and your own experience, the problem with going into Compulsion City and Escape City, is that those behaviors make you feel better for a few brief moments, but they're actually fooling you because it's only a matter of time before those uncanny obsessions show up again and again. The more you get hooked on the obsessions and use avoidance or do compulsions, the further away you get from doing the stuff that's important to you. Aren't compulsions so slippery? And yet, it's so hard to handle the urge to do a compulsion when you're swamped with overwhelming anxiety.

Karla, for example, had a fear of "something bad happening to her car," even though she has never had an accident and no one has ever broken into her car, scratched it, or done any damage to it in any way. Still, every time she parks her car at school, when going to grab frozen yogurt, or at her friend's home, this wave of fear shows up quickly, and she automatically walks around the car seven times in one direction, seven times in the other direction, and puts both her hands on the driver's door for 20 seconds. Only after completing this ritual is she able to walk away from the car towards her destination. A very well-ritualized compulsion, right? Doing this compulsion was very challenging for Karla because many times her friends were around and she felt anxious and embarrassed and didn't know what to do with her urges. Karla would pretend to be talking to them while walking around her car or she would tell them to go in first and wait until no one could see her doing her ritual. Sometimes, she was even late for her classes, for family gatherings, and important performances by her classmates. Karla also refused at all times to give a ride to her friends because she was scared about them seeing her doing this compulsion, even though she really wanted to hang out with them and just relax when driving.

Do you relate to Karla's struggle? Quite likely you do, because dealing with OCD episodes means that, on the one hand, there are unwanted thoughts floating in your mind and, on the other hand, there are things you may be doing to neutralize, get rid of, or minimize those obsessions. Here is something for you to keep in mind at all times and moving onward: Every time you get triggered, your nervous system naturally goes into an alert mode, and your overworking brain does its job to alert you by shouting at you and quickly organizing protective actions, like compulsive behavior, avoidant behavior, and asking for reassurance, even though there is actually not a reason to take any concrete action to protect you or start a war against obsessions—obsessions are just letters and words put together that pop up in your mind. But of course, your brain conjures up such bad scenarios that you may get hooked on them, making it challenging for you to not do a compulsion or avoidant behavior, and keep moving along with your day. Refocusing your attention as a skill is exactly what you need to do in those moments.

There are six steps to put into action the skill of refocusing your attention when feeling an intense urge to do a compulsion or engage in an avoidant behavior:

1. *Acknowledge you have an urge to do a compulsion or avoidant behavior.*

2. *Name your obsession:* here is [name].

3. *Disconnect from your mind.* There is no need to check why you're dealing with the obsession or how it's ruining this moment for you.

4. *Connect with your body.* Imagine that you are a tall, firm, and solid building, and you are so solid that even with high winds, rain, or hail, you remain steadfast. You can even wiggle your toes to remember you're there, present, and ready to make a choice. As a tall building, straighten your body, move your head from the left to the right, roll your shoulders, balance your body from one side to another, if you're standing, and, intentionally, take deep breaths and let the air out slowly.

5. *Connect with the outside.* Name and describe to yourself one thing you see, one thing you hear, one thing you smell, one thing you taste, and even one thing you can touch. Alternatively, you can choose something to focus on in your surroundings—anything you choose to name is totally fine. For example, you can tell yourself, "I see the whiteboard, I hear that noise in the patio, I smell the ink from the pen."

6. *Choose what to pay attention to.* Refocus your attention on what's important to you in the moment. If you're talking to a person, refocus on that person by listening carefully to the words, the looks of that person, and so on. If you're at school, and it's important for you to learn, focus on the discussion of the class, the teacher talking, and so on.

After you have named your obsession and decided to disconnect from your mind, you can repeat steps 4–6 as often as necessary. And when I say "as often as necessary," I really mean it. I promise you that when I get overwhelmed by my emotions and I'm so close to being jerked around like a puppet on a string, I follow these exact steps. They may look simple but they're quite powerful. Give them a try!

TRY THIS!

You don't need to wait for an OCD episode to start putting this unhooking skill into action—you can actually start practicing it right now!

Even if you're not experiencing an uninvited obsession showing up, or an urge to avoid or do a compulsive behavior, follow the above steps exactly as they are, and jot down how it goes for you. I know that it may feel weird, odd, and maybe even useless right now, and yet, I invite you to have a pinch of curiosity, give it a try, and see how it goes.

Jot down here how it went for you when you practiced refocusing your attention:

_____

_____

_____

_____

_____

_____

UNHOOK!

You have a new unhooking skill to add to your repertoire of ACT skills: refocusing your attention! The big plus of using this unhooking skill is that you can apply it to all those moments when you feel a strong push to do a compulsion, feel like wearing the fastest running shoes to Avoidance City, or when you're searching for someone to ask for accommodations. Every time there is a strong urge to move away from what you really want to be doing, that's a moment to stand up and refocus your attention! And as you have been doing in this section, go ahead and prepare for a bold move with your Choice Point graphic. Lastly, I want to encourage you to increase the number of times you're using the Choice Point graphic to three to four times a week. The more practice, the better!

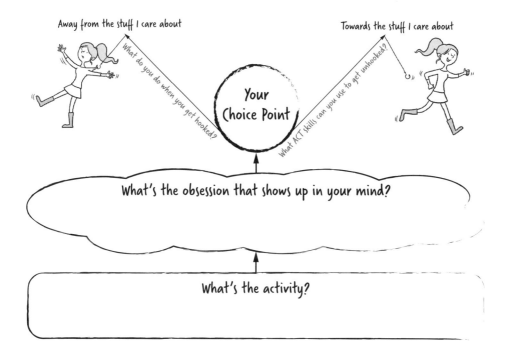

TIP FOR THE WEEK

Write down on sticky notes five of the most common obsessions you get hooked on. When you're done, you can either carry those notes with you in your pocket every day or place them in your bedroom where you can see them every day. If you're concerned about privacy, write a key word or a single letter as a reminder of the obsession. Notice what happens when you just let those notes be with those obsessions written down for seven days in a row!

CHAPTER 26

Hanging in There with Those Awful Feelings!

Patricia: Mom, I want to travel to Morocco because I would love to see the desert.

Patricia's mom: That sounds great and fun, just make sure you don't get sick with severe dehydration—it could happen.

Patricia: Mom, why would you say that?

Patricia's mom: Well, I love you and I just get scared about those things sometimes.

At some point in our life, we all get paralyzed with fear, flooded with anxiety, swamped with panic, and so on—your parents, my parents, you, me, and everyone around us. We're wired to experience all types of emotions, from the fun and exciting ones to the painful, uncomfortable, and annoying ones, no exceptions. And, when those obsessions show up, no matter how much you try to control them, it's so, so, so challenging because those intrusive thoughts come along with their allies—feelings of dread, fearfulness, creepiness, unease, and so on—that it's really hard for you to get unhooked. But, there is no need to let those feelings boss you around, because the more you practice *refocusing your attention*, or regrouping skills, the better you'll get at unhooking from those pesky obsessions.

We all experience fear and its related emotions in different degrees and at different times, like when taking a test, being in a dark place, going on a first date, or starting a new school—it's part of being human. But when we get triggered with obsessions, these nervous feelings are so loud that it's hard to ignore them and we easily get caught up in them. Do you ever wonder why those fearful feelings get so loud? Why every human being experiences them when they're so uncomfortable? To answer those questions, let's jump into a time machine and go back to ancient times.

First stop of the time machine: the Stone Age. Imagine that approximately one million years ago, back in prehistoric times, there are cave people doing their utmost to survive: preparing for weather changes, protecting the people in their tribe, searching for food and identifying what is edible, fighting against enemies, and of course hunting so they can have dinner at the end of the day. You're watching the cave people, and you see that suddenly one of them spots an enormous animal. How do you think this cave person feels in that moment?

Jot down your response here:

_____

_____

Second stop of the time machine: ancient times in which civilizations were springing up. Greeks, Romans, Egyptians, and others are figuring out how to live as organized a life as possible. They are forming villages, nations, and empires, in which people have different status. And from where you are in the time machine, you can see a Greek thinker, relaxing, holding a book, and sitting on a bench in a nice park. Suddenly a snake shows up. How do you think this Greek thinker feels and how does he react?

Jot down your response here:

_____

_____

Third stop of the time machine: the Middle Ages. This is when the printing press was invented, Christopher Columbus landed in America, and different kingdoms were trying to increase their territory, and getting into fights over and over. You see a group of soldiers preparing for a fight. What do you think they're feeling?

Jot down your response here:

_____

_____

Fourth stop of the time machine: the modern age. This is when people became increasingly interested in all types of art and discoveries, groups of people went from having kingdoms to having elected representatives, and some groups ended up with revolutions to have representative government. And, as you're getting a quick glimpse of this time in history, you see a king walking in the streets of a village and the people are very upset at him. How do you think he feels?

Jot down your response here:

_____

_____

Last stop of the time machine: contemporary times. Here you have groups of people not only working in factories, but inventing new forms of technology to produce all of the things we take for granted now, such as cellphones on which we can use Face Time, connecting with each other over huge amounts of space. And this time you see a teenager walking in the street and then a dog barks at him unexpectedly. How do you think the teen feels?

Jot down your response here:

_____

_____

And now, it's time to jump out of the time machine and bring yourself back to this workbook. What did you notice when looking at these different situations in different historical times? Quite likely you noticed that throughout the history of humanity, people have experienced fear, dread, terror, nervousness, and all types of related emotions because we're just wired to have all types of feelings, and many times, our body and nervous system automatically react without us doing anything. For example, when you feel scared or nervous, what do you notice in your body? Choose any of the phrases below that relate to what you go through:

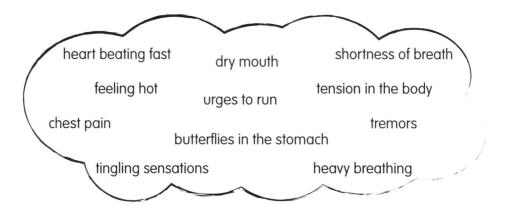

heart beating fast   dry mouth   shortness of breath

feeling hot   tension in the body
                  urges to run

chest pain   tremors
            butterflies in the stomach

tingling sensations   heavy breathing

And as you may recall from Chapter 4, "Why Do I Have to Deal with Fear?," the body, brain, and nervous system are doing their job, as they have been doing throughout the history of humanity. Depending on the situation, your body may go into a fight, flight, or freeze response.

The delicate part is that when dealing with OCD and anxiety, your brain—the same type of brain that everyone has had, from the cave people to the modern age—screams at you if anything looks dangerous, including images or thoughts of you dropping your cat from the 10th floor, getting stuck in an elevator, getting an awful grade, losing your mind, and other types of obsessions that are simply creations of your content generator machine, have nothing to do with danger, and have nothing to do with what you really care about. *Thoughts are thoughts, images are images, feelings are feelings, sensations are sensations, and none of that inside noise you go through is the same as reality. Even the most annoying urge is not the same as reality.*

Do you see how those overwhelming emotions may try to fool you because your mind is overreacting and playing tricks? It's only when you get hooked on those obsessions that come along with intense fearful emotions, or quickly agree with your brain, and do compulsions or run off to Avoidance City, that you get stuck in an OCD episode. Before you go any further, let's just be clear that your brain is just doing its job! So, what about saying something along the lines of:

> "Thank you brain! Thank you nervous system! Thank you for trying to take care of me and protecting me, but I got this one!"

And when those uninvited obsessions show up along with those overwhelming feelings, here is what to do: Watch them!

Yup, you read right. Feelings are sensations that show up in your body all the time. Sometimes they're low key, and other times are not so low key, but they are experiences you have, like many others—thoughts, dreams, sensations, and so on—no matter what your mind tries to tell you about them. The reality is that feelings have a limited lifetime. They have a beginning and an end, they don't last forever.

Regardless of the size of the emotion you're struggling with, we cannot stop our feelings even with our best efforts. Sometimes, you may be able to quickly reduce those fearful feelings and their variations by doing compulsions or avoiding a situation, location, or a person, but that's a very temporary response, because it's a matter of time before those emotions come up, and come up again and again.

TRY THIS!

Which one of the following feelings do you associate with your obsessions? Color or highlight those words that relate to you.

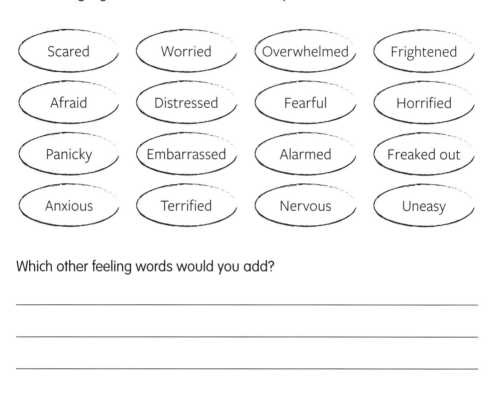

Scared   Worried   Overwhelmed   Frightened

Afraid   Distressed   Fearful   Horrified

Panicky   Embarrassed   Alarmed   Freaked out

Anxious   Terrified   Nervous   Uneasy

Which other feeling words would you add?

_____

_____

_____

_____

If you colored or highlighted one or all those words, you're not alone. All the clients I have worked with experience these emotions in different degrees, and it's also accurate for me to say that all of my clients do things to get rid of those feelings—such as doing compulsions, ritualized or non-ritualized, or avoiding a situation—to try to make sure that the feelings don't get bigger or out of proportion. It's natural, but the truth is that the more we try to run away from these unwanted emotions, the more intimidating they will become with time, even if in the short term they might shrink a little bit.

What about if instead of running or doing compulsions, you practice hanging in there with those feelings? While hanging in there, answer these five questions:

1. Where is the feeling in your body?

2. How big is it?

3. What's the color?

4. Does it have a texture?

5. Does it move in your body?

You don't have to like those feelings, and you do not have to want those feelings, but instead of fighting against them, you could just let them be and practice hanging around with them when they show up.

For example, Julie answered those questions like this:

1. Where is the feeling in your body? In my stomach, and chest

2. How big is it? Like the size of my shoe

3. What's the color? Blue, light blue

4. Does it have a texture? Not really

5. Does it move in your body? It moves back and forth between my chest and my stomach.

Your turn. Think about a recent OCD episode and answer the questions below:

Where was the feeling in your body?

_____

_____

How big was it?

_____

_____

What was the color?

_____

_____

Did it have a texture?

_____

_____

Did it move in your body?

_____

_____

When answering those questions, you're learning to hang in there with those fearful feelings and make room for them, and that's a core skill to practice and choose to practice over and over. There is no need to have a battle or a war against those scary emotions, but there is a need to notice when they show up, and turn down your fightonometer. You can do this!

UNHOOK!

Chapter by chapter in this section, you have been prompted to answer a key question: What do you want to do this week that matters to you? That's the same question I ask myself, almost on a daily basis. To be honest, it was only when I learned about what it really means to live a life based on my values that I learned the difference between doing whatever I had to do versus doing what truly matters to me. Not easy, but it's priceless to have those moments in which you're living the life you want to live. I hope that you have hundreds of moments like that in your life and that this workbook is a catalyst for you to continue dreaming, discovering, exploring, and creating the life you want to have!

Did you notice how the skills to get unhooked have grown from the beginning of the section to now? Keep moving and keep using your Choice Point graphic to make bold moves and put them into action! And by now, what about making bold moves every day?

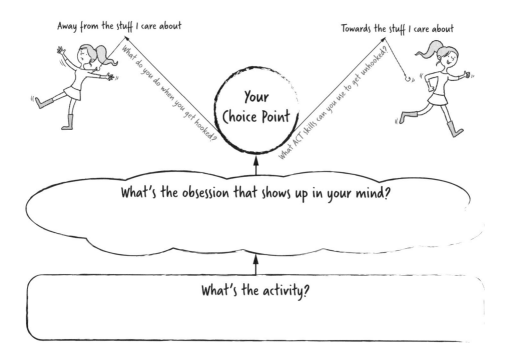

And as you might expect, when doing an activity that you care about, some annoying obsessions may show up accompanied by uncomfortable feelings, just like that. Using the illustration below, think about three uncomfortable emotions that may show up in your body when having obsessions and mark an "X" to localize them in the human figure. Color them and give them a shape and even a texture.

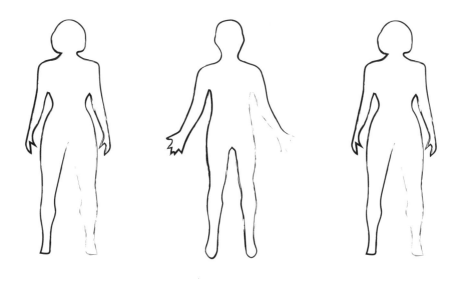

TIP FOR THE WEEK

Doing the stuff you care about comes along with all types of feelings: some of them are fun, like excitement, joy, and curiosity, and others feel yucky, like worry, fear, or even panic. The more you let those emotions run their own course, the less power they will have over you.

In addition to completing and putting into action your Choice Point graphic, practice watching how your emotion shifts without you doing anything besides watching it. Give it a shot!

CHAPTER 27

Agreeing to Get Out of Your Safety Country

Making room for doing the stuff you care about and getting unhooked from those annoying obsessions requires a very important unhooking skill: willingness. Willingness is your personal agreement to get out of safety country and move into living country while carrying with you the discomfort that comes along with your obsessions!

Let me share with you briefly what willingness looks like for Richard.

> Richard had an obsession about people stealing his knowledge if they touched him. Despite his efforts to avoid being touched by people, they often touched him on the shoulder to say hi, or his elbow would touch the elbow of another person when eating at the cafeteria, or when he was playing basketball his hands would touch the arm of another person, and so on. It was very challenging for Richard to manage his fear, and little by little, he came up with different reasons to avoid going to the playground, eating with others at the cafeteria, and hanging out with his friends at the mall, just to name a few of these avoidant behaviors. Richard felt embarrassed that he was unable to stop acting on his fear and couldn't go out with his friends. As the episodes continued to happen, Richard felt very sad because he loved spending time with his friends, wanted to be connected to them, and didn't want to miss out on the fun they were having.
>
> Richard genuinely cared about being a reliable friend, so, when putting willingness into action, he purposely ate lunch with two of his

classmates in the cafeteria, even though doing that meant that someone might touch his elbow.

Richard chose to feel his fear of *people stealing knowledge of him* as it was without fighting back, arguing against this obsession, or staying in safety country while making sure no one ever touched him. Richard didn't like having that horrible fear at all, but he realized that the more he got hooked on it, the less he was doing the stuff that mattered to him. Richard actively chose to do both, to live his values and have his fear come along for the ride! With time, Richard continued to practice choosing things that were important to him and moving along with that stinky fear. He also noticed that the more he practiced getting unhooked from that obsession, the more that he enjoyed himself. He felt more engaged, and even had the energy to take a piano class.

Willingness is the opposite of fighting against obsessions or powering through them. When practicing willingness, you actually do something totally active and different with those scary feelings: choosing to have them, accepting them, letting them be, letting them run their own course, and even choosing to cooperate with them. It's as if those scary feelings were a classmate from school that you don't get along with and when you're getting ready to have fun, here she is, the classmate that you don't like much, totally out of the blue, loud, trying to boss you around, and saying all types of provocative things. But, instead of talking back or proving that this classmate is wrong, you choose to let this uninvited classmate be on her own and do her own thing, and even when she follows you everywhere, you firmly do the stuff you care about doing because it's so much more important to you. With time, that unwanted classmate gets bored and does her own thing. Sometimes she goes back to bothering you, but then she forgets. And when you let her do her own thing and let your feelings of being scared run their own course, things get better.

Practicing willingness may feel weird in the beginning, but keep in mind that as much as those annoying obsessions try to boss you around, if you give into them, you will have less time, resources, and energy to take steps towards doing the stuff you care about.

Fighting against those fearful feelings is a lost cause, so watch out when you catch yourself in fighting mode!

TRY THIS!

To get unhooked from obsessions and to stop putting on your running shoes when you feel afraid, scared, anxious, or nervous, it's important that you start practicing willingness to feel all those feelings that you need to feel, including the uneasy ones, when it matters to you. You can have those feelings *while* you're doing stuff you care about. Willingness is about actively choosing to let those uncomfortable obsessions or overwhelming feelings or urges be background noise while you continue to take moves toward your values.

Here is a very important invitation for you: Make a commitment to open the door to those annoying obsessions, feelings, and urges when it matters to *you*! There's no one better than you to agree to get out of safety country!

After making a commitment, and saying yes to feeling what you need to feel, then ask yourself the five key questions you learned in the previous chapter, "Hanging in There with Those Awful Feelings!":

1. Where is the feeling in your body?

2. How big is it?

3. What's the color?

4. Does it have a texture?

5. Does it move in your body?

Before jumping to your Choice Point graphic for this week, let's look at how much you actually fight against the feelings that come along with OCD episodes. You may not even be aware of how much you let your feelings and urges boss you around. Let's find out!

What are the overwhelming feelings that come along with your obsessions?	Fightonometer: from 1 to 10, how much do you fight against this feeling? 1 = don't fight 10 = fight a lot	Are you willing to hang in there with this feeling rather than fighting it? Write down yes or no!

What did you notice when checking your fightonometer? Is there a particular emotion that you fight more than the others? And how was it for you to commit to having those feelings?

UNHOOK!

Ready to practice more unhooking skills? Dive into your Choice Point graphic for this week, at least once, and ideally three to four times if you're up for it. Prepare ahead to face those moments of doing the stuff you care about! Anticipate those hooks! Plan the unhooking skills you could use when getting triggered!

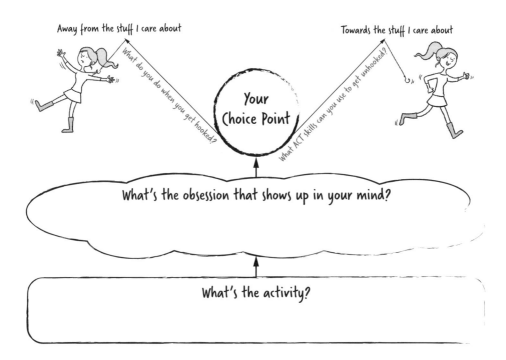

TIP FOR THE WEEK

Next time you find yourself fighting against an internal experience— obsessions, feelings, memories—check for yourself if having that fight is a move towards your values or away from them.

CHAPTER 28

Messing Around with Compulsions

Now that you have learned to let those uncomfortable emotions that come along with obsessions be, and are willing to get out of your safety country, it's time to do something about those compulsions. You and I know that trying to reason with compulsions won't do anything good in the long term, but messing with them will actually do the job of unhooking you from those loud obsessions.

Take a moment to think about those compulsions that you do when getting hooked on obsessions, and rank them based on how they affect your day-to-day life. The ranking doesn't have to be exact but just approximate, and focus on the compulsions you have been doing for the last 30 days.

Just as a refresher, keep in mind that compulsions are all the things you do to neutralize that pesky obsession of yours to make sure that you don't get out of your safety country. And watch out, because compulsions can be public or private, like telling yourself things that help you to feel better when having one of those obsessions—private compulsions—or walking around your car first one way and then the other—public compulsions. Just to clarify, I'm not suggesting that telling yourself cheerful things at times is a bad thing, I'm saying that telling yourself cheerful things to neutralize, reduce, decrease, or extinguish the fear that comes along with obsessions is a compulsion, and that's a different thing because it feeds into the OCD cycle and prevents you from living a full life.

For example, David had obsessions about not doing the right thing. He usually forced himself to think about a situation three times, and then he would tell himself, "I didn't do anything wrong, I didn't do anything bad, I did okay." Julie had fears of contamination. She had a ritualized compulsion. In Step 1, she put soap in her left palm, lathered each finger (thumb, pointer, middle, ring, pinky) of her right hand, and then repeated this for her left hand. In Step 2, she intertwined her fingers and then clasped her hands together. Then she lathered the back of each hand. In Step 3, she rinsed. Julie repeated Steps 1–3 three times and it usually took her 10–15 minutes every time. And if anything interrupted her ritual, she had to start over at Step 1.

To continue learning unhooking skills, in the table that follows, write down a word that reminds you of each compulsion and then rank it based on how much it affects your daily life.

Compulsions	Impact on your day-to-day life			
	Not much	A bit	A lot	Tons

Now that you have identified those compulsions and have ranked how they affect your day-to-day life, pick a ritualized compulsion that you're willing to work on for this week by modifying the order in which you complete it.

Staying with Julie as our example, she noticed that she really wanted to stop spending 10–15 minutes washing her hands and do other things, like relaxing, texting her friends, or watching YouTube videos. Julie decided to modify her compulsion to the following: putting soap in her left palm, intertwining her fingers, clasping her hands together, and then rinsing them. Julie also knew that modifying her compulsion was going to be difficult, so she made a point to remind herself that she could use the unhooking skills from Chapter 25, "Refocusing Your Attention":

1. Acknowledge you have an urge to do a compulsion.

2. Name your obsession: here is [name].

3. Disconnect from your mind.

4. Connect with your body.

5. Connect with the outside.

6. Choose what to pay attention to.

Julie was concerned about not being able to stop her compulsion right away. She used to refer to it as "the Imperius Curse," from Harry Potter, as if the compulsion had the power to direct her behavior. When modifying her ritual, Julie tried her best to repeat Steps 3–6 because she knew that if she got busy rationalizing her obsession or dwelling on it in her mind, she could easily give in to the compulsion. For Julie it was very helpful to detach from her mind by using her body: she first refocused deliberately on her breathing, then moved her body left to right a couple of times, and then focused her attention on the water running over her hands, the sound of it, and the temperature of it.

TRY THIS!

After choosing a ritualized compulsion you want to work on, check how you can modify the steps or order in which you complete it. You can use the form below to jot down the ritual and how you would like to modify it. In the top part you can write one word that reminds you of the compulsion and write your personal value.

If you decide to modify the _____ compulsion, what's the stuff that you care about that you're getting closer to? _____	
Describe how the compulsion looks now:	Describe how you want to modify it:

You just learned how to modify your rituals, and you can do this for any other compulsion that is affecting your day-to-day living. Messing around with your compulsions not only will disarm an OCD episode but it will also give you so much more time, energy, and resources to take action doing what's truly important to you!

UNHOOK!

How would you feel about selecting a particular life domain—family, friends, school, or community—and choosing two ritualized compulsions to modify? Afterwards, as you have been doing, complete a Choice Point graphic for a specific values-based activity you want to do, and when preparing for it, make sure to jot down "messing around with compulsions" as a skill to get unhooked—of course, only if it helps you to get close towards the stuff you care about.

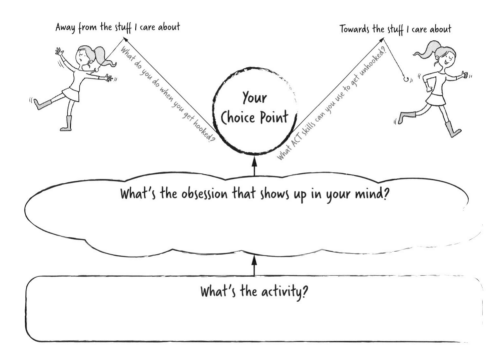

Away from the stuff I care about

Towards the stuff I care about

What do you do when you get hooked?

Your Choice Point

What ACT skills can you use to get unhooked?

What's the obsession that shows up in your mind?

What's the activity?

TIP FOR THE WEEK

Messing around with your rituals will get you so much closer to becoming the person, friend, relative, student, or community member you want to be. So, if your urge is to do A–B–C, messing around with it could be doing C–A–B in the moment. If fully modifying the ritual is hard, you could also take another mini step, such as delaying it, or making it shorter and shorter as you continue working with this book.

TAKEAWAYS!

Congratulations! I'm so happy you made it up to this point in the workbook and learned all the unhooking skills that I usually go over with my clients!

Imagine how much more space you can have in your life if you continue to use all these unhooking skills when the content generator of your mind does its thinking. As long as you're alive, your mind machine will always be doing its thing. Yet, in this workbook you're asked to practice a natural capacity you have as a human being: your capacity to choose and, in particular, your capacity to choose how to respond to those uninvited obsessions!

Now you know how to step back, unhook, and watch those obsessions for what they are: a bunch of words put together! And remember that if in any moment you find out that your mind is incessantly throwing at you all types of things, that's a great opportunity to practice one of your favorite unhooking skills, not to make the obsession go away, but to continue to watch it without getting hooked on it.

At the end of the workbook, in Appendix 3 you will find an unhooking log that you can use every week to practice these skills in your day-to-day life while doing what you care about with your feet, hands, and mouth. You can do this!

And keep in mind, if something feels too big, pause, take a deep breath, refocus your attention, and, when you're ready, try it again!

SPECIALIZED UNHOOKING SKILLS: EXPOSURE

Welcome to a new section of specialized unhooking skills!

In the last section, "Getting Unhooked!," you learned to watch your obsessions, watch them in action, say them in different ways, sing them, tease them, write them down, scramble them, refocus your attention, mess around with your compulsions, hang in there with different overwhelming feelings, and turn up your willingness to get out of safety country when doing the stuff that matters to you.

You did an amazing job learning and practicing many unhooking skills, getting familiar with your favorite ones, maybe even coming up with some new ones, and taking steps with your feet, hands, and mouth towards the things that you care about while carrying along those obsessions without letting them boss you around. Kudos to you!

If for whatever reason you didn't have a chance to practice the unhooking skills in Section 6, I would strongly recommend that you go back to that section, read each chapter, get familiar with them, figure out the ones you like, practice them, and check how they work in your day-to-day life. Reading about unhooking skills is one thing, but practicing them is a different thing. It's like the difference between reading about Bolivia and actually being in Bolivia, smelling the air, seeing Bolivian people in the street, and trying Bolivian food.

Now, it's possible that even with your best efforts using all those unhooking skills you learned in the previous section that you're still getting hooked on some obsessions that are highly resistant and have been reinforced hundreds of times with accommodations and compulsive or avoidant behaviors to the point that they have a life of their own.

This new section focuses on super-specialized unhooking skills—values-guided exposures—designed exclusively for those highly resistant obsessions. You will learn how and when to put into action these specialized unhooking skills and continue thriving in life.

Let's get you started on handling those highly resistant obsessions!

CHAPTER 29

A Word about "Values-Guided Exposures"

I don't know if among the many social media channels that are out there, you have a favorite or favorites. A few years ago I personally moved from Facebook to Twitter because I appreciate so much more the silliness and cleverness that people have when creating short messages. Here is a tweet I posted in 2018:

> Exposure is about approaching versus avoiding when it matters; it's practicing to have "x" and doing "y" when it matters; it's about moving towards what matters when it matters versus moving further away from what keeps us engaged. #ACT #ERP #behaviorism #values

I thought about this tweet when writing this chapter because it highlights the uniqueness of blending Acceptance and Commitment Therapy (ACT) and Exposure Response Prevention (ERP) together when working with OCD and anxiety episodes.

Let's break down this tweet a bit. If you remember from Chapter 2, "The Basics of Treatment and This Workbook," ERP is a very well-established treatment for OCD and anxiety struggles in general, and ACT, as a therapy approach, has demonstrated its effectiveness for treating OCD and anxiety in general in multiple research trials. Now you're going to learn more about exposures, but here is something important I want to tell you right away: In ACT, exposure practices are not about torturing yourself, pushing you further than you want to go, asking you to power through something you're scared about, or learning a technique and doing it like a robot. In ACT, exposure exercises are about you making a personal choice to face your fears—

whatever you're scared, anxious, or panicky about—in different situations and activities that matter to you, and that's exactly why they're called values-guided exposures.

In this workbook, everything you have been doing has been guided by your personal values because there is really no one better than *you* to find your Choice Point to put into action unhooking skills from your obsessions, hang in there with those intense emotions, and move along with your life.

Values-guided exposures are a continuation of the process of augmenting your unhooking skills for those highly resistant obsessions and turning down their volume in your day-to-day life.

Have you ever done yoga or have you ever tried to make the letter "T" with your body standing on one leg? What about putting down this workbook for a moment and trying? See if you can stand up straight on one leg with one foot on the knee of the standing leg and both of your arms extending out at shoulder level from your body for five minutes. What happened? Maybe it was easy at the beginning, maybe you fell down a couple of times, but if you continued doing it, you may have found your balance standing on one leg, just like when practicing values-guided exposures with highly resistant obsessions. You may struggle with some sticky moments, but if you continue choosing and choosing how and why to face your obsessions, you will find your Choice Point.

You know how to choose, it's within you. You just have to keep practicing to do it at all times!

Creating Your Values-Guided Exposures Dashboard

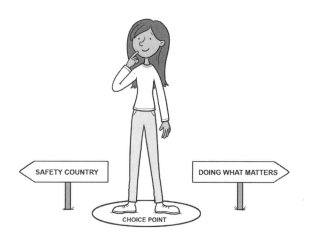

Some obsessions can be so persistent that they continue to come along with tons of fear, panic, and distress. You may wonder why this is still happening after you've put in all this work. Here is a short response: You're still hooked on those obsessions, taking them as absolute truths, and not as a regular creation of the content generator of your mind. And even though you don't want to, the association between those annoying words, images, and urges has also been strengthened hundreds of times with different actions such as compulsive, avoidant, or accommodating behaviors. This chapter will show you the first step to tame those resistant obsessions that invade your daily life: going back to check your personal values.

If you recall, in Chapter 15, "Doing the Stuff You Care About!," you listed your personal values in different areas of your life, created a values-action roadmap, and used it as a guide throughout every chapter in Section 6,

"Getting Unhooked!" Now that it's time to face your most resistant obsessions, there is no better way to begin than checking again what truly matters to you.

To start, imagine for a second that you're not dealing with OCD and you have the freedom to dream about all the stuff you care about. What would you choose to care about in different areas in your life—friendships, family, school, community, personal?

Remember that values are the qualities that are ultra-important to you, not to the adults around you. Values are not about wanting to feel happy or feel cool all the time because you don't have control of your feelings. Values are also not hopes about not having OCD, or wishes that other people will behave differently, because we don't have control over other people. Values are things you want to stand up for in your life, that give you meaning and purpose, and matter to you even when no one agrees with you. And because we work towards our values, we usually describe them with active verbs like "*protecting* the environment" and "*being* kind."

In the table below, write down your responses and check whether you're closer or further away from those values using the actionometer to rank your responses in the other column. Keep in mind that this activity is only for you so that you can check how you're living your life—no one will give you a grade or anything like that.

Life area: Write down your values	Actionometer: Think about your behaviors in this area over the last 30 days and mark an "X" where it corresponds
At school	← ─────────────────────────────── → Away from my values Close to my values

At home with family	
	Away from my values ←————————————→ Close to my values
With friends	
	Away from my values ←————————————→ Close to my values
As a community member (think about different groups you may belong to: spiritual, religious, sports, etc.)	
	Away from my values ←————————————→ Close to my values
Personal values	
	Away from my values ←————————————→ Close to my values

What did you notice when completing this activity? Are you closer or further away from what matters to you in those life areas?

Let's check how OCD episodes have continued to affect those life areas that matter to you over the last month. Check the table below and write down your responses for each one of those life areas. For example, Ameer, as a member of his religious group, wanted to try out a vegan dish because he really cares about *being healthy* and *protecting the environment*, but then he started having obsessions about germs, washing all the utensils, and monitoring who touched them over and over as compulsions. He started asking others if they had washed their hands when he saw them touching the refrigerator, separated his kitchen utensils from the rest of the family, and got really upset if someone didn't listen to him or answer his questions. For Ameer, OCD episodes affected his participation in religious celebrations, hanging out with his friends, or trying new restaurants. How has it been for you over the last 30 days? How are these OCD episodes still affecting your day-to-day living lately?

Life area	Write down different ways in which OCD episodes have affected this life area for you this last month
At school	
At home with family	

With friends	
As a community member (spiritual, religious, sports, etc.)	
On a personal level	

How was it for you when checking how OCD continues to affect your day-to-day life? Was your mind quiet or did your obsessions get to work and told you a bunch of stuff about what you can and cannot do?

Now that you have checked for yourself how you're doing with living your values and how OCD has affected your day-to-day living lately, the next chapters will help you to zoom in on those moments in which those resistant obsessions show up and show how practicing values-guided exposures could make a difference for you.

Ask yourself two questions: (1) what are all the uncomfortable or scary activities, people, feelings, images, and bodily sensations that you're still struggling with because of obsessions and end up avoiding, and (2) what are the compulsions you're still doing when taking those obsessions as absolute truths? Next, jot down the resistant obsessions that come along with them and why it's important for you to face all those situations in your life.

For example, Ameer came up with the following:

First question:

What activities, people, feelings, images, and bodily sensations am I still avoiding?

sleeping in my own bed

What's the resistant obsession that shows up in my mind?

If I sleep in my bed I may get some germs.

Why is it important to face this obsession in my life?

Because I want to be independent and live on my own at some point.

Second question:

What's the compulsive behavior I'm still struggling with?

rereading more than five times what I wrote down in my history class

What's the resistant obsession that shows up in my mind?

fear of making mistakes

Why is it important to face this obsession in my life?

Because I want to spend time doing fun things with my friends instead of checking many times what I write down.

After thinking a couple of moments on your responses, Use the values-guided exposure dashboard for resistant obsessions that follows.

VALUES-GUIDED EXPOSURES DASHBOARD
FOR RESISTANT OBSESSIONS

Jot down the activities, people, places, images, or physical sensations you have been avoiding that are important to you or compulsions you're still doing, and why it's important for you to face them in your life	How important is it from 1 to 10? 1 = low importance 10 = high importance
Example: Reading without rereading five times will help me to connect more with my friends outside of school and just hang out with them.	10
Example: Running during PE because being active is important for me.	8

Now that you have identified all the situations you are still avoiding, compulsions you're still engaging with, and why those people, situations, activities are important for you, make a note of this page or bookmark it, because this values-guided exposures dashboard for resistant obsessions is going to be your guide for the rest of the chapters in this section and you will need to come back to it multiple times. When things get rocky in our lives and we are dealing with highly resistant compulsions, there is nothing better than going back to our values.

And just in case, as sometimes happens to my clients when they are getting ready to put into action values-guided exposures, your mind is telling you right now, "I can't do this, it's too much. Do I really have to do it all at once?"—or anything along those lines—this is the moment to pause, notice those thoughts, and say to yourself "I'm having the thought..." or practice any of the other unhooking skills you prefer from Section 6, "Getting Unhooked!" You're in charge, and you're the only one who can choose how to respond to those annoying obsessions!

Let's move forward with planning your values-guided exposure exercises. Imagine for a second that you have been selected to be part of the swimming team in your school. You're excited to participate in it because you will get to practice with your friends, it's good for your health, and, on some days, you may be able to leave school early for swim practice. However, swimming practice involves swimming for 1.5 hours straight, and up to this point, you have swum continuously for only 30 minutes. How do you think that will be for you? Would you be able to swim for 1.5 hours straight? What do you think will be the most helpful approach? Perhaps you have already thought about this, but having small goals and swimming for longer and longer every time you swim will help you to reach the goal of swimming for 1.5 hours straight. In the same way, if there are things you have been avoiding and that task in hand seems enormous, you could break it down into smaller steps.

Breaking activities into small steps also applies for dealing with resistant obsessions. For example, Timothy really wanted to become a surgeon, but when reading or looking at videos or movies with scenes related to medical care his mind came up with violent images of dead and nearly dead people. Timothy got hooked on these images and was scared about being responsible for them. He ended up avoiding reading about medical stuff, visiting relatives in the hospital when they were sick, listening to anything related to deceased people, and wearing colors that are usually associated with hospitals. For a school project about careers, Timothy really wanted to be able to visit a hospital but it was very difficult for him to do so right away because of his obsessions. Working with his values-exposure dashboard for resistant obsessions, for this particular activity he started practicing by standing in front of a hospital for five minutes, four times a week, as a starting point.

Now you know that when organizing and arranging your values-guided exposure activities you are in charge, and you choose your pace and rhythm, and how to break down those big steps into small ones. Living a rich, meaningful, and purposeful life is not about how fast you run or how big your step is, it's about you choosing in which direction you move in and how you move.

Let's continue with these targeted unhooking skills for those resistant obsessions!

CHAPTER 31

Using a Situation for Values-Guided Exposures

As the title says, this chapter focuses on a very specialized unhooking skill: using a situation for your values-guided exposure.

You may wonder, why? Here is my response to you: Doing the things that matter to you, to me, and to everyone else is sometimes about approaching difficult situations that arise, including very scary and persistent images, thoughts, and urges. But, if you pause for a second, what's the alternative? To continue traveling to safety country when things get challenging? It's a natural behavior when we feel scared, but you and I both know what happens in your life when you take that path: OCD episodes get more frequent and you stop doing the stuff you care about. You and I also know by now that, as much as we hope to control what we feel and think, and to get rid of our fears, worries, and anxieties, we don't have a magic wand to make it happen. But we can choose every moment how to respond to those uncomfortable experiences we go through and keep living with our feet, hands, and mouth.

As scary as facing those situations may look, you're not tackling them in the dark, but with a lot of unhooking tools you have learned in this workbook. And just to make it crystal clear, approaching these situations is not about throwing yourself into something scary or jumping into a situation because your parents or therapist are forcing you to do it. Approaching these situations is about you choosing to get out of safety country because facing these situations matters to you.

Go ahead and make the best of learning this specialized unhooking skill!

PREPARATION TIME!

To start, go back to the values-guided exposure dashboard you created in Chapter 30, "Creating Your Values-Guided Exposures Dashboard," take a peek at the items you wrote, make a circle around the situations you have been avoiding or have been trying to manage with compulsions, and write a letter "S" next to each one of them so you can easily recognize them. Keep in mind that situations also include activities, people, and places you have been struggling with. Remember that you will need to go back to that list often, and repeat the values-exposure process over and over to continue moving forward with the stuff that matters to you. The good news is that every time you approach one of those scary situations, you're getting closer and closer to living your life!

Now that you have selected different situations and know how important each one of them is to you, select one that you are open and committed to facing, even while knowing that those obsessions may throw a tantrum, get louder, and insist you pay attention to them.

When looking at all the situations you have been avoiding or managing with compulsions in your values-exposure dashboard, it's really up to you to decide where you want to start—there is no particular order. If you find that some of the situations look too big, remember that you can break them down into small steps.

For example, Ameer from the previous chapter chose the situation "going for a sleepover at Mark's home" because he missed hanging out with his friend and playing video games. Ameer's obsession is "something bad may happen if I don't get in my bed by 6:30 p.m." When dealing with this obsession, usually Ameer asks his parents if everything is okay, retraces his steps from the hallway to his bedroom, retouches any item he touched in the hallway when walking toward his bedroom, and tosses his body left and right four times in bed.

Ameer decided to break his values-guided exposure for this situation into small steps, and wrote them in the form that follows.

Values-guided exposure step-by-step form

What's the situation I choose to approach for my values-guided exposure?	Why does it matter to me?
Sleeping at a friend's home after 6:30 p.m.	Because I value hanging out and connecting with my friends and family
What are the mini steps I'm willing to take for this values-guided exposure? Staying awake in my bedroom 10 minutes after 6:30 p.m. Staying awake in my bedroom 20 minutes after 6:30 p.m. Staying awake in my bedroom 30 minutes after 6:30 p.m. Texting Mark to schedule pizza and video games at his home on a weekend from 6:00 p.m. to 8:30 p.m. Texting Mark or another friend to schedule pizza and video games at his home on a weekend from 6:00 p.m. to 9:00 p.m.	

As you can see, Ameer broke down into tiny steps the situation he chose from his values-guided exposure dashboard, building up from being awake after 6:30 p.m. for 10 minutes to two-and-a-half hours as a way to hang in there with his obsession of something bad happening to him if he goes to bed after 6:30 p.m. Ameer wasn't ready to face that fear all at once, so he broke it down based on the time.

You can do the same if something looks too big to you. Depending on the task, you can break it down based on how close you get to it, the amount of time you engage on it, or even who you do it with. The most important thing to remember in overcoming OCD episodes is that you intentionally *choose* a situation that is truly important to you.

Your turn!

What's the situation I choose to approach for my values-guided exposure?	Why does it matter to me?

What are the mini steps I'm willing to take for this values-guided exposure?

Staying with Ameer, he also reread Chapters 25, "Refocusing Your Attention," 26, "Hanging in There with Those Awful Feelings," and 28, "Messing Around with Compulsions," to deal with the urge to retrace his steps, retouch items in the hallway, and toss and turn in bed. He made a point to keep in mind his plan that when he felt a wave of fear approaching, he would take a deep breath, roll his shoulders back and forth, use one of his favorite unhooking skills from obsessions—"I'm having the thought that something is going to happen to me"—and choose to focus on and describe his surroundings. Based on what Ameer read in his workbook, he knew that the more he fought against the urges, the anxious, fearful, and panicky feelings, and annoying obsessions, the worse they would get. And he remembered the steps to handle those intense emotions from Chapter 16, "Checking Your 'Fightonometer' When Doing Stuff You Care About":

1. Check if your fightonometer is on by recognizing what you're telling yourself: these feelings, thoughts, and urges are "bad, wrong, or a problem."

2. Check and describe to yourself what you're feeling or thinking or sensing by saying, "I'm having the obsession, thought, urge, image, feeling of..."

3. Check and describe to yourself what's happening in your body. For example, notice your breathing, your heartbeat, any areas of stress or discomfort.

4. Check what you're driven to do in the moment—what do you feel like doing?

5. Check if you can relax your body and take a deep breath.

6. Choose in that moment what's important to you: Is it worth continuing to fight with those uncomfortable experiences? If not, check and describe to yourself your physical surroundings.

You can use these steps not only when facing a situation for your planned values-guided exposure, but for any other values-guided exposure and when having strong urges to run to Compulsion City or Avoidance City. You can do it!

After checking if the situation from your values-guided exposure needs to be broken down into small steps, it's time to use the Choice Point graphic.

PLANNING YOUR VALUES-GUIDED EXPOSURE

The Choice Point was useful for all of your actions when learning all the different types of unhooking skills in Section 6, "Getting Unhooked!" In this chapter, you will also take advantage of the Choice Point graphic to plan your values-guided situational exposures.

After selecting the situation that you are willing to approach because it matters to you, list all the things you do that keep you hooked and list all the unhooking skills you can use when facing that situation using the Choice Point graphic.

Continuing with Ameer as an example, he has the fear of something bad happening to him if he stays awake later than 6:30 p.m. He decided to face the situation of *staying awake in his bedroom 10 minutes after 6:30 p.m.*, and when jotting down his Choice Point, it looked like this:

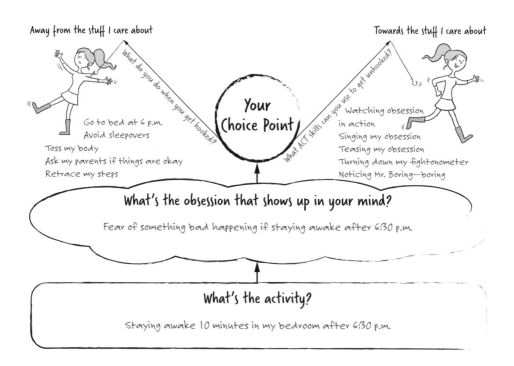

Away from the stuff I care about

Towards the stuff I care about

What do you do when you get hooked?

Your Choice Point

What ACT skills can you use to get unhooked?

Go to bed at 6 p.m.
Avoid sleepovers
Toss my body
Ask my parents if things are okay
Retrace my steps

Watching obsession in action
Singing my obsession
Teasing my obsession
Turning down my fightonometer
Noticing Mr. Boring—boring

What's the obsession that shows up in your mind?

Fear of something bad happening if staying awake after 6:30 p.m.

What's the activity?

Staying awake 10 minutes in my bedroom after 6:30 p.m.

Jot down your Choice Point for the fearful situation you want to tackle. Here are some reminders for you when filling it out: you get hooked when taking the obsession as an absolute truth—instead of just a thought that your mind comes up with—and end up doing things that take you away from the stuff that really matters to you like compulsions, avoidance, or asking for reassurance. Ameer got hooked on his obsession when asking his parents if everything is okay, retracing his steps from the hallway to his bedroom, retouching any item he touched in the hallway when walking toward his bedroom, and tossing his body left and right four times in bed.

At the bottom of the Choice Point, write down the situation you chose to approach, in this case the situation you want to focus on for this values-guided exposure. Choosing to deal with uncomfortable situations just because a workbook or your therapist says you should is not a good enough reason to get out of safety country, but approaching situations because they matter to you and help you to be the person you want to be, that's a different story.

Naturally when choosing to take steps towards what matters to you, those unsolicited obsessions may pop up, so write them down in the thought bubble. And as you have been doing, jot down all the unhooking skills that will help you to take steps towards your personal values.

If it helps, you can always go back to Section 6, "Getting Unhooked!," to remember all the unhooking skills or take a look at the Unhooking Log in Appendix 3.

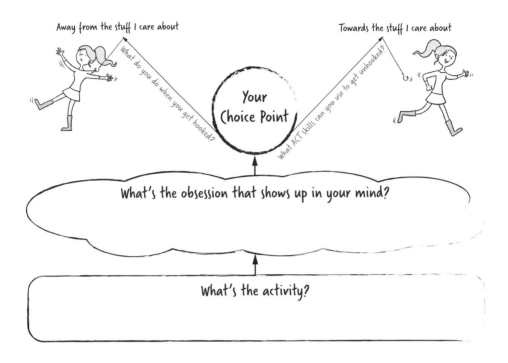

Using the Choice Point really helped Ameer to organize his exposure exercise, and it can definitely help you too!

FINDING YOUR CHOICE POINT IN ACTION

Using the Choice Point graphic as a planning tool for your values-guided exposure exercises will help you learn how to handle OCD episodes and also serves as a reminder that, wherever you are in your day-to-day life, you can choose how to respond to those fearful moments that come in life, regardless of whether it's an OCD episode or not.

And if your mind is like my mind, it's natural that now that you're getting ready to approach a situation you care about, the content generator machine of your mind may come up with some loud obsessions. Your body may react, intense feelings may show up, and you may have strong urges to put on your running shoes and run as fast possible into safety country. But pause for a second and ask yourself: What's the price you pay if you do avoid that situation you care about? What happens to your life? Do you become the person you want to be?

It's actually in those moments when approaching a values-guided exposure of a situation that matters to you that your Choice Point is right there, in that precise moment when you are wrestling with those overwhelming obsessions and choosing between two options: (1) doing all types of avoidant responses and moving further from your personal values, or (2) choosing to have that loud obsession and letting the fear, distress, and anxiety run their own course, as you continue to move forward with your feet, hands, and mouth towards what you truly care about. You are the only one who can actively make this choice in those moments of struggle.

When Ameer was approaching the situation of staying awake for 10 minutes after 6:30 p.m. his mind came up with fearful thoughts: "It feels wrong; you're attracting bad things to you." He felt a big knot in his stomach and urges to force himself to sleep, call his parents right away, and ask them if everything was going to be okay. But Ameer knew that the more he continued to do any of those behaviors, the less chance he would have to connect with his friends, and he was tired of the old soundtrack of his mind. So, he took a deep breath and then described his bodily reactions that he learned in Chapter 26, "Hanging in There with Those Awful Feelings!": "I'm sensing a knot in my stomach, it's heavy, and it doesn't move." Ameer wasn't running away from his fear of something bad happening to him by staying late after 6:30 p.m., he was actually describing the feeling. Ameer also decided to call his obsessions "the broken record story," and when having a thought related to them, he said to himself, "That's the broken record story." Ameer repeated these skills a couple of times, breathing and breathing, and still choosing to stay awake for 10 minutes after 6:30 p.m.

When doing values-guided exposures, do your best to not talk yourself out of the exposure or start fighting against the obsession or power through it. Check if your fightonometer is on, and just do your best to ride the wave of fear! If you find yourself fighting those obsessions, questioning them, labeling them as "wrong" or "bad," or tensing your body, intentionally take a deep breath, relax that body area, and practice again having those feelings and thoughts as they come and use one of your favorite unhooking skills.

Doing values-guided exposures and moving in the direction that you know in your heart you want to move is finding your Choice Point in real life, and in particular in those moments of struggle. No one better than you to make that choice in your life!

REFLECTING ON YOUR VALUES-GUIDED EXPOSURE EXERCISE

After completing your values-guided exposure practice, it's helpful to debrief on how it was for you. Use the form below to reflect on it. And because you will use this form multiple times, there is a blank one in Appendix 4 at the back of the book and you can also download and print copies as needed from www.jkp.com/catalogue/book/9781787750838.

When Ameer completed this form, it looked like this:

What was the value that drove your exposure exercise? Connecting with my family and friends	
What exposure exercise did you do? Staying awake after 6:30 p.m.	
Check your fightonometer! How much did you fight the obsession and the annoying feelings that came along?	_____X_____ 0 1 2 3 4 5 6 7 8 9 10 didn't fight fought a lot
Did you get closer or further away from the stuff you care about?	_____X_____ Away Towards
Did you do any public or private compulsive behavior or did you ask for reassurance? If your answer is yes, describe the behavior, and think about what unhooking skills you could have used in those moments.	None of them. I had the urge to ask my parents if things were going to be okay, but didn't. I took deep breaths multiple times.

Now, your turn!

VALUES-GUIDED EXPOSURE REFLECTION FORM

What was the value that drove your exposure exercise?

What exposure exercise did you do?	
Check your fightonometer! How much did you fight the obsession and the annoying feelings that came along?	0 1 2 3 4 5 6 7 8 9 10 didn't fight fought a lot
Did you get closer or further away from the stuff you care about?	Away Towards
Did you do any public or private compulsive behavior or did you ask for reassurance? If your answer is yes, describe the behavior, and think about what unhooking skills you could have used in those moments.	

And before we finish this chapter, let's clarify when to use a situation for values-guided exposure, so you know when to do it!

QUICK TIP TO USE A SITUATION FOR VALUES-GUIDED EXPOSURE

Think for a moment about all those times in which you went into avoiding mode or ended up doing compulsions in a situation that you truly care about. Moving forward, I want to encourage you to look at those moments as opportunities to practice a values-guided exposure using that particular situation. Managing your resistant obsessions can feel unnatural and tedious at first, especially before you begin enjoying the freedom that will come from dropping the fight against them. But as you keep choosing to do values-guided exposures, you will slowly notice that every effort you're putting into facing your fears is completely worth it.

And you should be aware that doing values-guided exposures doesn't have to be boring or serious, when it's already hard to handle those annoying obsessions. You can be totally creative in putting together your values-guided exposures. For example, if a person has obsessions about having a different sexual orientation, exposure activities could be seeing movies or music videos with attractive people from that sexual orientation, wearing outfits of that particular orientation, or going out to places that are frequently visited by people of that particular sexual orientation.

Keep moving and moving, and keep living and living!

CHAPTER 32

Using Your Imagination for Values-Guided Exposures

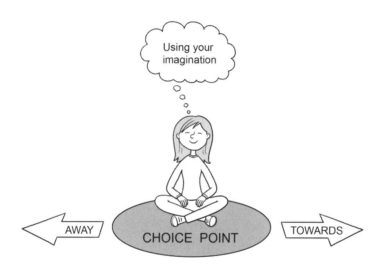

Doug was reading a Twilight story about vampires for school, and after completing his reading, out of the blue he had an image of himself as a vampire. The image was so real and alive that Doug got scared and quickly replaced it with a nice and positive image of himself in his house at the dinner table. Doug knew that it was a weird image, and yet he couldn't stop feeling scared every time it popped into his head. He got so scared that he ended up telling his parents they were in danger because he might harm them.

Doug was struggling with an obsession that showed up as an image, and despite his best efforts to keep hanging out with his parents or friends, he got hooked on this obsession for over three months and started avoiding anything that brought him into contact with people he was afraid he may harm, such as family dinners, playing sports, and going skateboarding with his friends at the weekend.

Doug will benefit from using another specialized unhooking skill—values-guided exposure—to tackle that resistant obsession of becoming a vampire. Because this obsession is showing up as an image, using his imagination for it will be super-helpful.

PREPARATION TIME!

It's hard to face something you're scared of, and it would be totally understandable if you were thinking seriously about stopping reading this book right here. But here comes a big but: Facing your fears and practicing exposures in the service of doing what you care about with your feet, hands, and mouth is one of the biggest gifts you can give yourself. And by now, you also understand that going into Compulsion City or Avoidance City, or asking others for accommodations, takes you in the opposite direction from your values—instead of walking north, you end up walking south.

As you did in the previous chapter, go back to your values-guided exposure dashboard from Chapter 30, "Creating Your Values-Guided Exposures Dashboard," and take a peek at all those resistant images you have been avoiding and struggling over and over, despite your best intentions to use the unhooking skills you learned in this workbook. Make a circle around each one of them and write a letter "I" for "image" next to each item.

For Doug, using his imagination for a values-guided exposure involved imagining himself as a vampire and visualizing as many details as possible, like the color of the clothing he is wearing, his facial expression, what his body looks like, what he is doing in the image—attacking his parents—and other characteristics of himself as a vampire.

In order to maximize and make the best use of your imagination, you may need to write down a narrative to face some of these images you're scared of. If you decide to write a script for imaginal exposure, here are the key elements for it: (1) write it in the first person ("I"); (2) write it using the present tense; (3) include as many details as possible, so the image of that particular situation is vivid, but without overdoing it (you're not writing a novel or an essay); (4) make sure to include your worst fear; and (5) don't include any compulsions or avoidant behaviors in the writing.

Use the form below to write down your script for using imagination in a values-guided exposure. This form is also imaginal exposure.

VALUES-GUIDED EXPOSURE FORM: USING YOUR IMAGINATION

What's the image I choose to approach for this values-guided exposure?	Why is it important to me to practice having this image for this values-guided exposure?

Write down a narrative that describes your worst fear, describing things you will see, hear, touch, smell, and even taste. Make sure to write this narrative down in the first person, using the present tense, and don't include any compulsions or avoidant behaviors as part of it.

After writing down the narrative for your imaginal exposure, you can record it on your cellphone and listen to it on a daily basis. And just to make it crystal clear, listening to this recording is not about getting rid of the obsessive thoughts, but practicing having them. If you need more forms for other values-guided exposures using your imagination, there is a blank one in Appendix 5 or you can download further copies from www.jkp.com/catalogue/book/9781787750838.

PLANNING YOUR VALUES-GUIDED EXPOSURE

Now that you have learned the nuts and bolts of using your imagination for putting values-guided exposures into action, let's go back to the Choice Point graphic. At the bottom of the Choice Point, write down the obsessive image you chose to approach based on your values-guided exposure dashboard.

Doug's Choice Point graphic looked like this:

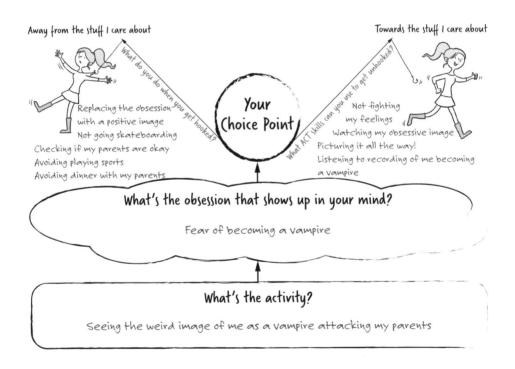

Your turn!

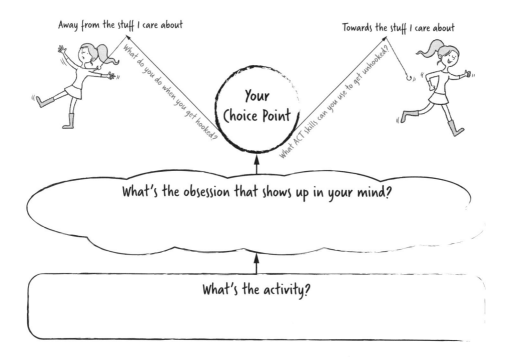

FINDING YOUR CHOICE POINT IN ACTION FOR YOUR VALUES-GUIDED EXPOSURE!

When putting into action this values-guided exposure using your imagination, you know that your obsessions are going to show up, kicking in and trying to get you hooked, like a bully does at school, and that's when you have your Choice Point: Do you give in to avoidance, compulsions, or asking for reassurance, or do you move forward with your values?

You're not encountering your obsessions in the dark any longer—you have many unhooking skills to choose from and put into action in a moment of struggle. Every moment you find yourself struggling with a potential OCD episode is an opportunity for you to practice *choosing* your behavior. In those moments of choice, checking in with yourself about what's really important for you can give you the strength to withstand the difficulties that come in that moment and point you in the direction *you* want to take.

You know that the more you fight having all those annoying feelings that come along with that image, the worse they get. And by fighting, I mean replacing the image, arguing back with it, telling yourself key words or sentences to reduce your anxiety, and any other distractions that reduce your discomfort temporarily but that shrink your day-to-day living.

Always keep an eye on your fightonometer!

REFLECTING ON YOUR VALUES-GUIDED EXPOSURE EXERCISE

After you have put into action your values-guided exposure, there is nothing better than pausing, reflecting, and checking how you did when facing your fears. In the end, it's all about learning!

VALUES-GUIDED EXPOSURE REFLECTION FORM

What was the value that drove your exposure exercise?	
What exposure exercise did you do?	
Check your fightonometer! How much did you fight the obsession and the annoying feelings that came along?	0 1 2 3 4 5 6 7 8 9 10 didn't fight fought a lot
Did you get closer or further away from the stuff you care about?	Away Towards

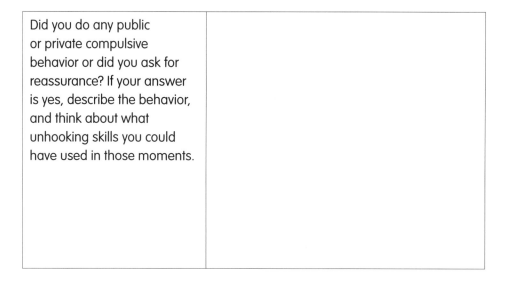

Did you do any public or private compulsive behavior or did you ask for reassurance? If your answer is yes, describe the behavior, and think about what unhooking skills you could have used in those moments.	

QUICK TIP FOR USING YOUR IMAGINATION FOR VALUES-GUIDED EXPOSURE

I suggest that you use your imagination for a values-guided exposure when your obsessions are images popping into your head and it's not possible to use a situation for a values-guided exposure.

For example, if you have an obsessive image of stabbing your siblings or people you care about, or getting a terminal illness and slowly dying, it isn't possible or desirable to create situations for those obsessions in which you literally stab someone, or contract a terminal illness. It is helpful, therefore, to use your imagination for values-guided exposure. However, you could also organize values-guided exposures using situations that still trigger those obsessions, such as holding a knife next to the person you're scared about stabbing or watching videos of people who have contracted the illness you're scared of.

In Chapter 34, "Mixing Up Your Values-Guided Exposures!," you will learn more about combining different types of values-guided exposures to continue to learn to respond to your obsessions flexibly while you keep moving forward with your life.

And now, let's get you moving into another type of values-guided exposure!

CHAPTER 33

Using Your Body for Exposures

Dr. Z.: How are you doing today Reid?

Reid: Dr. Z., there is a problem.

Dr. Z.: What happened?

Reid: I have a tremor in my hands and legs...that's a sign of multiple sclerosis. I may have it...

Reid took his bodily reactions as a sign that he was contracting a neurological disorder and, as a result, refused to go for hikes, didn't participate in physical education class at school, spent time googling multiple sclerosis and its symptoms, and checked constantly for signs of it in his body.

Reid's obsession was quickly activated when he experienced particular bodily sensations: a knot in his stomach, his heart beating fast, a tremor in his arms, and a loss of strength in his muscles. Even though Reid went to see three different doctors for a medical checkup, and they all denied that he had multiple sclerosis or any sign of it, he couldn't let it go.

Reid was having an ongoing battle with this obsession, got hooked on it, and didn't see he had a choice about how to handle it. Despite his efforts, he went along with compulsive behaviors. However, if Reid learnt to do values-guided exposures using his body, he would get better and better at having those uncanny bodily sensations without getting bossed around by them.

Let's see how this looks like in this chapter.

PREPARATION TIME!

As you know by now, the starting point for any values-guided exposure exercise is to go back to the values-guided exposure dashboard. This time make a circle around situations or activities you have been avoiding because doing those activities usually comes with uncomfortable and distressing bodily sensations that have been quite annoying and that lead you to get hooked on the obsession. Make sure to write a letter "B" next to each item just to remember that you can practice values-guided exposures using your body. And lastly, choose one of those activities you're willing to face with the purpose of doing what matters to you.

Let's move to the Choice Point graphic to plan and prepare for this exposure!

PLANNING YOUR VALUES-GUIDED EXPOSURE WITH THE CHOICE POINT

Grab your pencil or pen and start jotting down the situation you choose to approach or prepare for, the obsession that comes up right away, your go-to responses to neutralize, minimize, or get rid of the obsession, and all the unhooking skills you could use to move towards what you care about.

For example, Reid wanted very badly to go back to taking PE classes because he missed being active and being silly with his classmates. He decided to name his obsession "Mr. Lost Cause," write it down on a flashcard, and carry it with him all day. When Mr. Lost Cause popped up in Reid's mind, he visualized Mr. Lost Cause sending an email and he deleted the email without opening it. But Reid also knew that some physical sensations were very triggering for him, so he needed specialized unhooking skills for values-guided exposure exercises using his body so he could get better and better. In therapy, we discussed the following options: jumping up and down with a heavy jacket so Reid could notice any fluctuation of his heartbeat for a few minutes and doing 100 sit-ups to help him to get better at feeling the knot in his stomach. Reid's Choice Point looked like this:

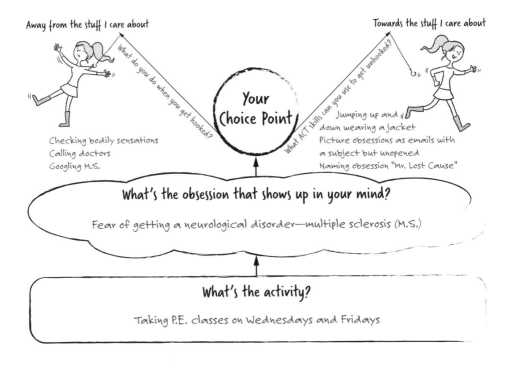

Up for it? If you need suggestions for using body-based exposure, think about what other activities you usually do as part of your daily life that may come along with similar physical sensations that are bothering you, but are not associated with OCD episodes. For example, if having shortness of breath is a trigger for having an obsession, then exercises like running up and down the stairs, and jumping up and down, could be helpful. The most important thing is not to simply throw out random things to do but to do exposure exercises that are part of your regular life. Now, sometimes you may need extra exercises to use your body. For example, if you're dealing with an obsession about not swallowing properly and it feels wrong, an exposure exercise could be swallowing fast, then slowly, and vice versa.

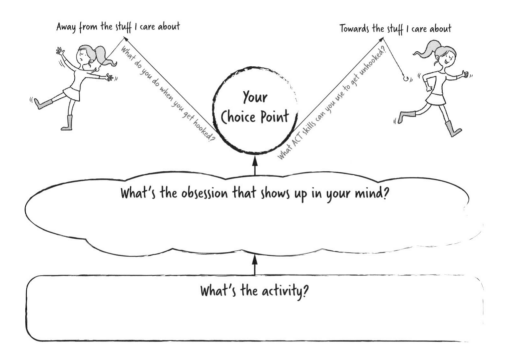

FINDING YOUR CHOICE POINT IN ACTION FOR YOUR VALUES-GUIDED EXPOSURE

Kudos to you for using the Choice Point graphic to plan and prepare your upcoming values-guided exposure focusing on bodily sensations! As you know, one of the main purposes of this workbook is to invite you to find your Choice Point in real life and in particular when you're facing these triggering situations and those resistant obsessions.

Here are my recommendations about how to handle those overwhelming sensations that show up in the midst of a triggering situation: (a) take a deep breath; (b) use one of the unhooking skills you learned in the previous section—saying, singing, picturing, teasing, watching the obsession, and so on; (c) describe to yourself what you feel—the sensation in your body, color, texture, movement; (d) drop your fightonometer all the way; (e) refocus in the moment; and (f) let the thoughts, sensations, emotions, and urges to do compulsions follow their own course.

You don't have to follow those steps in order but just remember them when you are facing a triggering situation and repeat them as needed while continuing to face that situation. Finding your Choice Point is key to choosing the stuff you care about and doing the stuff you care about. Go for it!

REFLECTING ON YOUR VALUES-GUIDED EXPOSURE

Your values are your compass, and facing your fears as you do with exposures is about taking steps toward what matters to you. Take a moment to debrief on this last values-guided exposure exercise as a concrete step toward living the life you want to live, not the one that those resistant obsessions push you to live!

VALUES-GUIDED EXPOSURE REFLECTION FORM

What was the value that drove your exposure exercise?
What exposure exercise did you do?

Check your fightonometer! How much did you fight the obsession and the annoying feelings that came along?	0 1 2 3 4 5 6 7 8 9 10 didn't fight fought a lot
Did you get closer or further away from the stuff you care about?	Away Towards
Did you do any public or private compulsive behavior or did you ask for reassurance? If your answer is yes, describe the behavior, and think about what unhooking skills you could have used in those moments.	

QUICK TIP TO USE YOUR BODY FOR VALUES-GUIDED EXPOSURE

You can use your body for values-guided exercises when your OCD episodes start with unwanted bodily sensations or concerns about particular bodily sensations like tremors, hyperventilation, breathing, and so on.

In the last three chapters you have learned how to use situations, your imagination, and your body for values-guided exposure exercises as concrete steps to handle those resistant obsessions and continuing living the life you want to live. The next chapter will show how you can make the best use of these unhooking skills so you can get better and better at noticing those unsolicited obsessions and simply recognize them as the products of the content generator machine of your mind.

CHAPTER 34

Mixing Up Your Values-Guided Exposures!

Quick question: Have you tried fruit smoothies? Do you have a favorite one?? I personally love a delicious green smoothie. The one I usually drink has kale, cucumber, green apples, spirulina, and a bunch of other ingredients. It doesn't look good at first sight, but, to be honest, it's very tasty and healthy, so I drink it as much as possible.

What's interesting about smoothies is that if you try the ingredients individually, they do have a flavor on their own, but when you combine them, some of them just taste better. Mixing things up can sometimes make individual components better and that applies for values-guided exposures too. When you face what you fear using a specific situation, your body, *and* your imagination for values-guided exposures, you're augmenting your super-choosing skills and getting better and better at doing the stuff that truly matters to you.

For example, Maria, a 13-year-old, has a fear of contracting germs. She gets very anxious when having this obsession, feels her heart beats ultra fast, and has been avoiding visiting her aunt at a hospital because of this resistant obsession. Maria could do a mix up of values-guided exposures like this:

- *Using a situation:* visiting a waiting area at a hospital so she can connect with her aunt later on.

- *Using imagination:* writing, reading, recording, and listening to an imaginal script about contracting germs so she can be caring when visiting her aunt at the hospital.

- *Using the body:* jumping up and down to practice feeling her heart beating fast, as happens when her obsessions show up, so she can show her care for her aunt by visiting her.

Now that you have a sense of how you can put together a situation, your imagination, and your body when doing values-guided exposures, take a peek at your values-guide exposure dashboard and see which activities you can mix up. Some items will benefit from all three different ways and others may be better using only two, or one, and that's okay. Mixing up your values-guided exposure activities is not a rule or a necessity, but a suggestion that will help you to get better and better at handling those resistant obsessions.

To start, write down an item from your values-guided exposure dashboard that may benefit from mixing exposure practices:

_____

_____

Which values-guided exposure exercises did you come up with to mix up?

Using a situation:

_____

_____

Using your imagination:

_____

_____

Using your body:

_____

_____

Give it a go, and as usual, make sure to reflect on this values-guided exposure practice.

VALUES-GUIDED EXPOSURE REFLECTION FORM

What was the value that drove your exposure exercise?	
What exposure exercise did you do?	
Check your fightonometer! How much did you fight the obsession and the annoying feelings that came along?	0 1 2 3 4 5 6 7 8 9 10 didn't fight fought a lot
Did you get closer or further away from the stuff you care about?	Away Towards
Did you do any public or private compulsive behavior or did you ask for reassurance? If your answer is yes, describe the behavior, and think about what unhooking skills you could have used in those moments.	

TAKEAWAYS!

At the end of this section on values-guided exposure exercises for those ultra-resistant obsessions, I just want you to know that I really value how hard you have been working to get out of safety country and back into living your life! I know it's not easy, but if you made it to this point in the workbook it is because you're committed to stop the ongoing chain of OCD episodes you have been dealing with. You're on track to live the life you want to live!

At times handling obsessions will be more manageable than at others, and occasionally, despite your best efforts, you may end up doing compulsions, avoiding a situation, or asking others for accommodations. We all have moments like that, and we all have moments in which we make moves away from the stuff we care about. If you encounter those moments, I want to invite you to ask yourself a key question: When things go bad in a given moment, are you willing to start again in the next moment and go back to making moves towards the stuff that truly matters to you while handling those annoying obsessions? I hope your answer is yes, because you may be surprised by all the amazing things that come when you put your choosing skills and personal values into action. There's no one better than you to choose, moment after moment, and no one better to choose when to face your fears, why facing those fears matter to you, and how to do it.

As you have read in this section, practicing values-guided exposures is not about torturing yourself but about introducing you to specialized unhooking skills to handle those resistant obsessions that are overwhelming and as hard to let go of as if they came with Velcro attached to them.

Make sure to work through all items from your values-guided exposure dashboard and keep track of your steps by filling out the debriefing form after each one of the values-guided exposure exercises.

Do your best to keep practicing them and continue making bold moves in your day-to-day life towards what's important to you. Living your life is choosing your values, and choosing your values doesn't mean anything until you act on them! Keep moving towards creating the life you want to have!

MOVING FORWARD WITH YOUR LIFE

Can you believe that you've reached the last section of the workbook? Congratulations on all the effort you've put into completing the exercises, practicing your Choice Point, trying different unhooking skills, and getting better and better at choosing. Tons of appreciation to you!

As challenging as those annoying obsessions may look, the amazing news is that there is no better time than *right now and at this moment* to begin choosing to live your values, ideals, dreams, and aspirations for your future. Your teenage brain is flexible, capable, and open to new experiences, and as long as you continue to practice those choosing skills, surprising things may come your way.

Give yourself praise for all the work you have been doing, and get ready to learn about extra helpers to handle the obsessions that the content generator of your mind throws at you, including practicing values-guided exposure on-the-go and as the need comes up in life, finding an ally at home or school, treating yourself with care, and staying in the moment instead of staying in your head.

Let's get moving!

CHAPTER 35

Discovering Values-Guided Exposures "On-the-Go"

Obsessions don't turn up on schedule and you can't use a planner to determine when they will interrupt your day—they just come, they just show up. And moving onward, you can approach them as they come, and as values-guided exposures "on-the-go."

Norah, for example, after realizing how compulsive, avoidant, and reassurance-seeking behaviors got her hooked on the obsessions, and learning different types of unhooking skills, started doing more things on-the-go, as they just happened and because they just happened. For instance, after school Norah's friends invited her to go for a hike. In the past, because of her fear of having a rushed feeling and the possibility of cursing at her friends, Norah would have said no, but this time she actually said yes. When hiking, Norah continued to use private unhooking skills like picturing her obsession—fear of cursing at others—as the baby character from *The Incredibles*, watching it scream, checking its fightonometer, and noticing thoughts like "I shouldn't be feeling this, this is a wrong feeling." She took a deep breath to ground herself, and continued walking step-by-step along with her friends, and along with her obsessions.

Norah was practicing values-guided exposures on-the-go because when she got invited to go for a hike, she didn't have that item in her values-guided exposure dashboard and didn't have a chance to add it either. This is what I call "living your life," and that's why I call these exposures values-guided exposures on-the-go!

When living your life, it's natural that your overworking mind is going to come up with all types of unwanted content because that's what minds do when doing their job. Your mind anticipates dangers, even though the danger it anticipates may be far from what's actually happening outside your skin. The mind, as usual, is a very cautious device we all carry with us.

Here is my invitation to you: just keep moving with your feet, hands, and mouth toward what matters. And when encountering unexpected twists and turns as they happen in life, use your favorite unhooking skills, not to get rid of those unsolicited obsessions, but to continue to practice having those thoughts without getting hooked on them.

You can use the form below to keep track of the different exposures on-the-go you encounter in a week.

VALUES-GUIDED EXPOSURE ON-THE-GO TRACKER

Write down the different situations you unexpectedly encounter in a given week and check how you did with your fightonometer!

Day 1: Values-guided exposure on-the-go

0	1	2	3	4	5	6	7	8	9	10
didn't fight									fought a lot	

Day 2: Values-guided exposure on-the-go

0	1	2	3	4	5	6	7	8	9	10
didn't fight									fought a lot	

Day 3: Values-guided exposure on-the-go

0	1	2	3	4	5	6	7	8	9	10
didn't fight									fought a lot	

Day 4: Values-guided exposure on-the-go

0	1	2	3	4	5	6	7	8	9	10
didn't fight									fought a lot	

Day 5: Values-guided exposure on-the-go

0	1	2	3	4	5	6	7	8	9	10
didn't fight									fought a lot	

Day 6: Values-guided exposure on-the-go

0	1	2	3	4	5	6	7	8	9	10
didn't fight									fought a lot	

Day 7: Values-guided exposure on-the-go

0	1	2	3	4	5	6	7	8	9	10
didn't fight									fought a lot	

Wherever we go and whatever we do, we will all experience fear, anxiety, worries, or panic at some point, whether that's because of OCD or not. But the more you practice values-guided exposures, whether they're planned or on-the-go, the better you will get at facing fearful moments as they come up in life. All your work, efforts, and energy are going to pay off.

CHAPTER 36

Tracking Your Progress towards Living Your Life to the Full

Everyone on this planet has weird thoughts popping up here and there, sometimes a lot, sometimes a little—that's just what the content generator machine of our minds does. So you may wonder, what happens if you have a new annoying obsession? That's a possibility because neither you nor I have control of what shows up in our minds, but we do have control and the capacity to choose how to respond to those loud thoughts.

As you have learned in this workbook, having an obsession is not what leads to an OCD episode, but putting on your running shoes to run into Avoidance City or Compulsion City, or asking for reassurance from others, is what quickly shapes it into an OCD episode.

Think back to when you started reading this workbook and all that you have learned. Take a peek at Chapter 13, "Checking the Costs of Getting Hooked," and check for yourself what has changed for you in those areas in your life:

Life areas	Then...	And now, what has changed?
In my friendships, OCD has affected me by:		
At school, OCD has upset me by:		
At home, OCD has caused me to:		
In my hobbies, OCD has influenced me to:		
In relationship to myself or feelings about myself, OCD has led me to:		

How was it for you completing the above form?

You have accomplished so much up to this point! From the first to the fourth section of this workbook, you learned about obsessions, different explanations of why people deal with OCD, specific treatment options, how ACT, exposure, and the Choice Point graphic can be super handy for you, what maintains an OCD episode, and how your brain is constantly overworking by sending you all types of signals about what's scary in an attempt to protect you. In the fifth section you took the time to figure out the real stuff you care about and how every action we take takes us either further away or closer to our personal values. Then in the sixth section you learned, tried, and put into action a bunch of unhooking skills to handle those uninvited obsessions, and figured out how to pay attention to your fightonometer. And you didn't stop there, because in the seventh section, you went beyond all the unhooking skills and practiced values-guided exposure exercises using a situation, your imagination, or your body.

Congratulations on reaching this point in the workbook and getting back into your life! I know it has taken a lot of time, persistence, effort, and dedication to get to this point. I hope you take a moment to pause, appreciate your hard work, and feel proud of what you have accomplished so far!

CHAPTER 37

Finding an Ally!

When writing this workbook, I allotted two days a week in my schedule for writing. I started writing and continued on until it was time to submit the manuscript to the publishers. Usually, every two to three hours I took a mini-break, stretched, had a bite to eat, maybe a piece of dark chocolate, and then went back to writing. I honestly didn't know how much I enjoyed writing until I started taking on some writing projects, and to be honest, I think that writing has definitely helped me to be a better therapist. I get excited about translating the work I do with my clients into books or written material.

But completing writing tasks confirmed for me that there is something else that is very important that comes along with these projects—and that's the important realization that I couldn't have finished this project, or any other one, without the encouragement of my friends, family, and colleagues. There were many times when I would text them with random requests for their support, and after a couple of minutes I'd receive texts back with cute emojis, sometimes long, detailed responses, other times short responses, but every time I put myself out there asking for a hand, there was someone on the other side supporting me.

And that's what we do in friendships and relationships with people we care about: we show that we care and we show up for others. We don't need hundreds of those relationships but only a few that are there for us. Sometimes, just one friend can make a difference for us. I call them "allies." Allies can be your buddies, friends, siblings, classmates, or neighbors, you name it. And they can also be your parents or caregivers. As cheesy as it sounds, having people that care about us makes a difference in our day-to-day living!

Here is a text I sent to my friend a month before finishing writing this workbook:

Me: I'm going to start writing, can I please ask for a hug?

Friend's response: Tons of abrazos [hugs]!

Nice, right? Humans are social beings. We need to feel a connection to other people, and when we feel connected, that's a powerful motivation for us! Being connected can be as simple as texting a caring message, checking in with people to see how they are doing, letting people know how we're doing, and so on. That's why sometimes we're more likely to go on a trip together than alone, hang out at a mall with others rather than solo, or go to the movies with friends than on our own. We are wired to connect!

Below is what you could do.

To start, list the friends, relatives, or classmates that you feel comfortable sharing about OCD. It doesn't matter if there are lots of people or just few of them, but jot them down below.

List your potential allies to support you to keep moving forward with your life:

1. _____

2. _____

3. _____

4. _____

5. _____

Now, remember that when an OCD episode occurs, one way of handling those pesky obsessions is by asking others to do or not do things for you (asking for accommodations or reassurance). For example, Jamila had an obsession about people stealing her knowledge and leaving her dumb, so sometimes she asked her classmates to look on the other side of the room when completing a test or doing homework at school. At home, at the end of the day, Jamila asked her mom to quiz her for an average of 5 to 10 minutes per subject, to make sure that no one stole her knowledge.

Of course, Jamila's classmates and her mom didn't want her to be stressed out, so they went along with her requests. But as you know by now, those accommodations only work in the short term. Even though Jamila may have felt better in the moment, in the long term she continued to live in safety country, which kept her OCD episodes going and going, and going and going again. She got so busy managing those OCD episodes that she didn't have a chance to just chill out with her friends and forgot how to enjoy their company.

So, when asking others for support, it's important for you to be clear about ways in which others can support you. Be specific with them, instead of people guessing about what they have to do or say when you get anxious. Some of my clients like to show their unhooking logs to their parents once a month, ask a friend to remind them that the "fear will run its own course if they don't do anything," ask parents to remind them of doing a values-guided exposure once a month, or ask relatives and friends not to answer reassurance questions, just to name a few examples.

It's really up to you to think of ways in which others can be supportive with you when dealing with pesky obsessions or overwhelming fear. Write down ways in which the people on your list could support you:

1. _____

_____

_____

2. _____

_____

_____

3. _____

_____

_____

4. _____

_____

_____

5. _____

_____

_____

Now, go over the list of your potential allies and the list of ways in which they could support, then choose one person and come up with three specific ways (or even just one way) they could support you:

Ally's name:

_____

Specific support activities:

_____

_____

_____

And just to avoid misunderstandings, below are some recommendations for you to share and to clarify with your ally:

- Your ally is a support person and not the OCD police.

- Be specific about what type of support you would like, when you want it, and what's helpful to you and what's not. For example, "It would be nice if once a week you check in with me about how I'm doing with handling my obsessions."

- If you decide to ask one of your allies for support when practicing one of those specialized unhooking skills, like exposure, be specific about it. For example, "I choose to attend Chemistry class because I want to learn interesting stuff, but my obsessions about having bad feelings and mixing positive and negative energy make it hard. Can you come with me? And if you're okay going, and I ask for your help, please don't tell me things like 'It's going to be okay' because that's reassurance and it doesn't help me in the long run. But you can say, 'You're doing your best right now and it's really up to you to choose how to respond to this anxious feeling.'"

And now use the lines below to jot down a draft of what you would ask this ally to do in supporting you in moving along with your life!

_____

_____

_____

_____

_____

_____

CHAPTER 38

Treating Yourself with Kindness!

When I was close to the end of writing this workbook, I ended up getting a terrible cold. Despite my best efforts, I could only stay awake for two to three hours and then I needed a nap. I'd wake up again for two to three hours and then take another nap, and so on. The nights were the worst because I became a coughing machine and sleeping was almost impossible for weeks.

Unexpected things happen that are out of our control, and for many of us, our minds, like a content generator machine, take us to places that we don't want to go. My mind came up with thoughts along the lines of "My publishers will be upset with me; the teens won't like the workbook; I won't get better from this cold; will I be sick for the whole year?" and so on... And, when these unplanned things crop up, it's natural that the content generator machine of your mind will scream at you with obsessions that may seem so real and so true that, at times, you may end up getting hooked on them as I did when getting hooked on all those thoughts when having a cold.

It's natural, we all do it—we all get hooked from time to time. But at times your mind also may come up with loud judgments like: "You're not getting better; nothing is working for you; you're going backwards; you're not working hard enough." Your mind can't help it. You cannot make your mind behave better, but instead of taking your mind so seriously—as if it's a bossy boss—you can choose how to respond to those judgments.

When you hear your mind coming up with all those criticisms, negative self-judgments, or blaming thoughts—either because of those pesky obsessions or because in the fear of the moment you engaged in compulsive, avoidant, or reassurance-seeking behaviors—those are the precise moments to practice kind behaviors.

Yup, you read that correctly. Kind behaviors are not only actions from you towards your friends, but they are also from you to you!

Why not pause for a moment and try the exercise below? Read the directions first, and then give it a try!

If you're sitting down or standing up, try to straighten your back, drop your shoulders, and press your feet gently against the floor. Next, recall a moment in which you had those loud criticisms showing up in your mind, and as you bring that moment into your mind, take a deep breath, make room to watch those judgment thoughts, and see if you can come with a name for them. Don't worry if it's not a perfect name, but just a name for you to recognize them, and imagine them as little ghosts on top of your shoulder screaming and criticizing you. See if you can watch them, and with gentleness, notice the feelings that come up and the sensations that show up in your body. As you continue to notice, slowly bring your hand towards your body in a gesture of bringing caring, support, and kindness towards yourself, and place your hand wherever you feel a sensation or a feeling—perhaps it's your stomach, your chest, your head—but gently let your hand rest there. And, as you let your hand rest there, keep in mind that your struggle is part of being alive, of being human, and not a sign of something being wrong with you.

How did it go for you? I hope you put this exercise into action just as a way to practice kind behaviors towards yourself. And if you want a recap of it so you can practice it anytime throughout your day, below are the mini steps listed for you to practice self-kindness:

1. Take a deep breath.

2. Notice those self-critical thoughts.

3. Name them (e.g. here is my harsh voice; Queen Judgy is here).

4. Unhook from them using one of your favorite unhooking skills (from Section 6).

5. Place your hand on your body where you notice your hurt or distress and make room for that feeling without trying to push it away, fix it, or get rid of it. Or if you prefer, you can even softly hug yourself with caring.

And, because practicing kind behaviors is a skill that can be developed, practice Steps 1–5 a couple of times, as you do with any other skill.

There is no need to be harsh with yourself when getting hooked on obsessions or if you find yourself running into safety country. And, even if your content generator machine is coming up with hundreds of criticisms at the speed of light, remember, there is no winning against the mind, so no need to prove it wrong, come up with a positive thought, or replace thoughts. But, you can always *choose* to respond to that mind noise with kindness, exactly as you do when you see your friends struggling, with the difference that this time it's about practicing kindness from you to you!

CHAPTER 39

Getting Out of Your Mind and into Your Life

Here is the beginning of a Saturday evening for me:

Dr. Z.: I really want to lie down on the sofa, watch the new Spider-Man movie, and just enjoy the evening!

Content generator machine: Did you finish the laundry? What about the paper you have to write? Did you notice the dust on the TV? Remember you need to call your mom; how many days more until Christmas? I miss the sunny weather. There is something different with my smoothie today. Halloween kitty, where are you?

Dr. Z.: Oh boy, I just want to watch the new Spider-Man movie. I may need to fire my brain for 2 hours and 15 minutes while watching the movie.

Any reactions to the above interaction between what I wanted to do and what my wonderful mind—a content generator machine—came up with? Have you been there? Isn't that interesting that our minds don't take a break, vacation, or holiday? They just keep going on and on and on, nonstop. Our minds don't take vacations, don't know about holidays, and they don't get paid either. They just keep moving, 24/7. The reality is that our minds are just doing their job. They're doing their own thinking and thinking!

Your mind, like my mind, creates all types of thoughts, funny ones, hypotheses, questions, judgments, worries, rules, memories, images, fantasy thoughts, dreams, storytelling thoughts, obsessions, and so on...and while your mind keeps doing its own thing, you are not your thoughts, you just have them. And just because you think it, it doesn't make it so.

No matter how certain and secure your mind seems to be, a thought is just a thought. A thought isn't reality, and obsessions are not your enemy. What about if, along with all the skills you have learned in this workbook, you learn two more: staying in the moment, and getting out of your mind and into your life!

After finishing this chapter, close the workbook, and practice for yourself to see how much you have taken from it.

Here is what to do to practice *staying out of your mind and getting back in your life*: When your mind wonders about anything, and a thought, any type of thought, pops up, see if you can catch the thought with a hand gesture, in the same way as you catch a spider. And, as if you're holding the thought as a physical thing, just put it in your pocket. An alternative gesture is that you catch the thought, and then press it against your body as if you're placing the thought in your skin. It's really up to you which hand gesture you prefer to use. There is no right or wrong way to do this exercise—it's more important you give it a try. When catching those thoughts with a hand gesture, you can name them if you like—here is judgment; here is Ms. Perfect, Mr. Sassy, jealous thought, etc.—and then go back to focus on what you're doing in that precise moment.

Sometimes, you may notice your thoughts coming really fast, and in those moments, hang in there with those fast and wondering thoughts, just do any of the physical gestures you choose, and then choose what you really want to pay attention to.

If paying attention, answering, and dwelling on all those thoughts that show up in your mind helps you to take steps toward your values, go for it. But if those thoughts are mere distractions and take you away from what's happening in front of you and the stuff you care about, there is no need to engage with them at all. In those moments, take a deep breath, and just do your best to go back to paying attention to what you were doing or pay attention to your surroundings by describing five things you see, hear, smell, taste, and touch.

For example, Steven was hanging out with his friend at a party of the swimming team, and while chatting with his group of friends, the content generator machine of his mind came up with the obsessive thought of "I need to say this sentence correctly so it feels right." Steven noticed the thought, knew that this thought had shown up before in his mind, and so he called it "the feeling good thought." He then took a deep breath and chose to pay attention to his external surroundings. He noticed the tone of voice of each one of his friends, the smell of the soil after the rain, the taste of the slice of pizza he'd just had in his mouth, the texture of his jeans against his hand after pressing it on them, and observed the colors of the sky on the horizon.

Steven described all those observations to himself while continuing to watch his mind, and he decided to not respond to that mind noise. There is really no need to mind your mind at all times!

Give it a try as you continue moving forward with your life!

CHAPTER 40

Finding Your Choice Point in Life

Here is the beginning of one of my sessions with a client:

Dr. Z.: Hello Meredith!

Meredith: Hi, Dr. Z. How are you doing this week?

Dr. Z.: Good, thanks. Just complaining about the cold weather as usual.

Meredith: Yeah, I know you don't much like the winter. Did you have a good weekend?

Dr. Z.: Yeah, it was a relaxing one. Had a yoga class to start the day.

Meredith: That's nice. Did you like your yoga class?

Dr. Z.: To be honest, my yoga class was a challenging one because I couldn't find balance all the time. In some of the postures I just fell down; in other postures I could manage while still wobbling; and in others I was able to hold the pose steady. It was challenging to find that moment when my whole body came together.

For the last 15 years, doing yoga has been an incredible asset in my life. Every Sunday I'm at the yoga studio practicing 26 postures: 13 standing ones and 13 on the ground. I honestly never know how each class is going to go because every posture is an invitation to find balance, coordination, and equilibrium in my body, and sometimes I have to hang in there with those "feelings of giving up right away."

If you practice any sport, whether it's swimming, running, cycling, playing football, or any other sport, you know that that sport is also an invitation for you to pay attention to how you move your body, the strength you have in different areas, the tension points you struggle with, and how you also have to hang in there with those moments when you feel like stopping right away.

It's in those moments when we feel like stopping, running away, dropping our sport practices, and so on that we face our Choice Point. Do we keep moving through these challenging moments or do we stop? No one can respond for us, no one can choose for us. It's our Choice Point. It's your choice, it's my choice.

From the beginning to the end, in every chapter of this workbook, you have been prompted to use the Choice Point graphic. I didn't do that to bore or torture you but to actually help you to get familiar with a single graphic that shows you how every time you have an obsession you can handle it by doing something that takes you closer to or further away from the stuff you care about. And, a big take-home message is that making moves towards or away from what you care about applies to everything you do, from sleeping, yawning, studying, hanging out with friends, and so on... Everything we do is a step toward or away from what's truly important to us.

The Choice Point graphic was a way to remind you of a capacity and core skill that you already have but may have forgotten or didn't know how to apply when dealing with annoying obsessions: your capacity to choose.

Ever since you were born, your capacity to choose was there. This may sound silly to you, but think about it for a bit: When you were a kid, your parents chose many things for you, from what you wore, to what you ate, the school you went to, and the time you went to bed. But all that time, your choosing skills were naturally developing, and little by little, you practiced them in different circumstances. For example, maybe you remember that you discovered you didn't like broccoli and didn't want to eat it, no matter how it was prepared. Or maybe after playing with many toys, you realized you liked one more than another and spent more time with it. Maybe still, among the many movies you watched, you chose one with your favorite movie character, and later on, with all of the music you heard, you listened to the songs you liked best. I could continue going on with examples, but the reality is that ever since you were born, there was within you a capacity to choose—it is a core inner skill you have.

And one of the most important things that I hope this workbook has accomplished is to encourage you to notice the Choice Points you face in your day-to-day living, as those obsessions, fears, anxieties, and worries come your way. You don't need to carry the Choice Point graphic with you at all times, but you do need to keep your eyes open to all those moments when you encounter your Choice Point and have to choose between organizing your life around pushing down, controlling, and avoiding fear or living your life your way. It's exactly in those moments when you have that pull, that struggle, that there is, right there, your Choice Point, and it's exactly in those moments in which the best thing you can do is to choose. No one better than you to choose!

The End!

Here we are, at the end of the workbook. You made it—woohooooo!

I truly hope that this workbook and all the skills you learned working through it were helpful to you in dealing with those annoying obsessions and moving along with your day-to-day living. You may want to have this workbook available to you so you can pick it up at any time, and try the activities again, because sometimes you may just need a refresher of any of the skills to keep living your life.

Do you remember how it was for you when you started reading this workbook? It's possible that those obsessions were bossing you around and pushing you to do this, that, and the other! But now something has changed: You have the skills to choose where you want to go with your mouth, hands, and feet. You can pursue what matters to you and hang in there with those obsessions because they're not in front of you directing your behaviors like little dictators any more.

It's been such a treat to put together this workbook as part of an action I took toward my personal value of disseminating treatments that work. I did my best to show you how you can handle those pesky obsessions using all of the ACT unhooking skills moment-by-moment. And now, it's really up to you to choose how to continue doing what you truly care about, even when taking small steps—they eventually add up!

Close to the end, I hope that, if nothing else, you've learned that having obsessions is not a sign that something is wrong with you or that you're broken, but an indication that you're just wired to think a lot.

And lastly, there are two things I encourage you to continue doing. First, invite those obsessions to come along on the ride of your day and make sure to check you fightonometer: Are you fighting them or letting them be? And second, make your life bigger than your obsessions. I know you can do it—you can—and you have all the skills to do so!

I wish you an amazing and rich life in every step you take!

Warmly,

Dr. Z.

P.S. Don't forget to check the website www.actbeyondocd.com to keep practicing how to live the life you want to live even when those obsessions show up!

Appendix 1: Choice Point Graphic

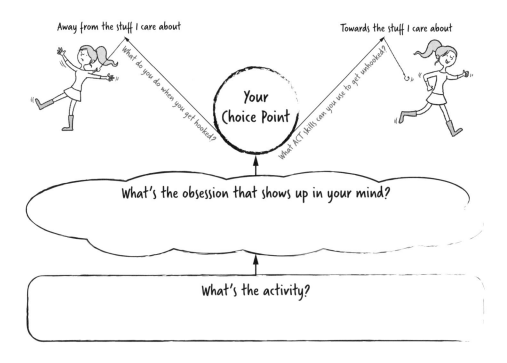

Away from the stuff I care about

Towards the stuff I care about

What do you do when you get hooked?

What ACT skills can you use to get unhooked?

Your
Choice Point

What's the obsession that shows up in your mind?

What's the activity?

Appendix 2: Values-Guided Exposure Step-by-Step Form

What's the situation I choose to approach for my values-guided exposure?	Why does it matter to me?

What are the mini steps I'm willing to take for this values-guided exposure?

Appendix 3: Unhooking Log

Here is a list of all the unhooking skills that you learned, and I hope you continue to move forward in your life doing the stuff you care about while applying these skills to your day-to-day life. Do your best to fill it over a week and review it too. You got this!

Unhooking skill	Monday	Tuesday	Wednesday	Thursday	Friday	Saturday	Sunday
Picturing and giving it a name							
Watching your obsessions in front of you							
Putting your obsessions into action							
Saying your obsessions							
Singing your obsessions							
Teasing your obsessions							
Writing down your obsessions							

Scrambling up your obsessions							
Refocusing your attention							
Hanging in there with those awful feelings							
Agreeing to get out of safety country							
Messing around with compulsions							
Delaying compulsions							
Checking your fightonometer							
Using a situation for values-guided exposure							
Using your imagination for values-guided exposure							
Using your body for values-guided exposure							
Finding an ally							
Finding your Choice Point							

Appendix 4: Values-Guided Exposure Reflection Form

What was the value that drove your exposure exercise?	
What exposure exercise did you do?	
Check your fightonometer! How much did you fight the obsession and the annoying feelings that came along?	_____ 0 1 2 3 4 5 6 7 8 9 10 didn't fight fought a lot
Did you get closer or further away from the stuff you care about?	_____ Away Towards
Did you do any public or private compulsive behavior or did you ask for reassurance? If your answer is yes, describe the behavior, and think about what unhooking skills you could have used in those moments.	

Appendix 5: Values-Guided Exposure Form: Using Your Imagination

What's the image I choose to approach for this values-guided exposure?	Why is it important to me to practice having this image for this values-guided exposure?

Write down a narrative that describes your worst fear, describing things you will see, hear, touch, smell, and even taste. Make sure to write this narrative down in the first person, using the present tense, and don't include any compulsions or avoidant behaviors as part of it.

Appendix 6: Values-Guided Exposure On-the-Go Tracker!

Write down the different situations you unexpectedly encounter in a given week and check how you did with your fightonometer!

Day 1: Values-guided exposure on-the-go

0	1	2	3	4	5	6	7	8	9	10
didn't fight									fought a lot	

Day 2: Values-guided exposure on-the-go

0	1	2	3	4	5	6	7	8	9	10
didn't fight									fought a lot	

Day 3: Values-guided exposure on-the-go

0	1	2	3	4	5	6	7	8	9	10
didn't fight									fought a lot	

Day 4: Values-guided exposure on-the-go

0	1	2	3	4	5	6	7	8	9	10
didn't fight									fought a lot	

Day 5: Values-guided exposure on-the-go

0	1	2	3	4	5	6	7	8	9	10
didn't fight									fought a lot	

Day 6: Values-guided exposure on-the-go

0	1	2	3	4	5	6	7	8	9	10
didn't fight									fought a lot	

Day 7: Values-guided exposure on-the-go

0	1	2	3	4	5	6	7	8	9	10
didn't fight									fought a lot	

Appendix 7: Answers to Activities

CHAPTER 1: THE BASICS ABOUT OCD

Activity: Crossword

Answers: Down: 1. Unwanted; 2. Fear; 3. Compulsions. Across: 4. Short term.
5; Impulses; 6. Aggression.

CHAPTER 2: THE BASICS OF TREATMENT AND THIS WORKBOOK

Activity: Wordsearch

```
Z  O  S  U  F  S  O  G  N  P  U
A  Y  E  M  F  R  J  I  R  B  Y
N  B  C  H  O  I  C  E  H  W  G
A  J  B  E  J  W  R  D  E  Z  B
B  U  S  Q  R  N  Q  S  D  E  O
B  Q  E  V  B  U  M  O  O  B  O
P  E  K  Z  Q  A  S  U  H  V  W
V  F  V  Q  B  O  W  O  I  H  R
A  H  Y  U  S  T  R  W  P  X  E
N  T  C  A  H  N  R  Q  R  X  R
U  B  I  Y  I  Q  B  M  K  A  E
```

CHAPTER 9: UNINVITED URGES

Activity: Word scramble

Answers: 1. Obsessions; 2. Fear; 3. Urges; 4. Obsessive images; 5. Unwanted
thoughts.

CHAPTER 15: DOING THE STUFF YOU CARE ABOUT!

Activity: Matching activity

Answer key: activities are petting a dog, eating ice-cream with friends, searching new music, and watching movies with my best friend; values are being caring, having courage, helping others, and being trustworthy.

CHAPTER 24: SCRAMBLING UP YOUR OBSESSIONS

Activity: Poem unscrambling activity

Answer key: Tell [me]
What is it [you]
[plan] to do
With [your] one wild and [precious] life?

Appendix 8 : Further Resources from Dr. Z.

WEBSITE SPECIALIZED IN ACT AND OCD

The website www.actbeyondocd.com offers materials, e-books, exercises, handouts, and worksheets for you to use to continue practicing the application of ACT skills for OCD. On this website you can sign up to a quarterly newsletter which distributes new free resources as they are created.

BOOKS WRITTEN BY DR. Z.

Zurita Ona, P. (2018) *Escaping the Emotional Roller Coaster: Acceptance and Commitment Therapy for the Emotionally Sensitive*. Australia: Exisle.

Zurita Ona, P. (2017) *Parenting a Troubled Teen: Deal with Intense Emotions and Stop Conflict Using Acceptance and Commitment Therapy*. Oakland, CA: New Harbinger.

BOOK CO-AUTHORED BY DR. Z.

McKay, M., Fanning, P., and Zurita Ona, P. (2011) *Mind and Emotions*. Oakland, CA: New Harbinger.

THERAPY SERVICES WITH DR. Z.

Dr. Z. is the founder of the East Bay Behavior Therapy Center (EBBTC), a boutique therapy center specialized exclusively in empirically based treatments, including Acceptance and Commitment Therapy, for children, teens, and adults struggling with OCD, trauma, anxiety disorders and related conditions, and mild to moderate emotional regulation problems. Dr. Z. developed an Intensive Outpatient Program (IOP) for OCD and other anxiety conditions that offers intensive exposure treatments—15 hours a week—for children, teens, and adults.

More information at www.eastbaybehaviortherapycenter.com.

PROFESSIONAL CONSULTATION AND TRAININGS WITH DR. Z.

Dr. Z. offers ongoing consultation to professionals interested in learning the applications of ACT for specific struggles such as OCD, anxiety, trauma, and emotion regulation.

Acknowledgments

I finished writing this workbook on a winter dawn, with a loud central heater running in the background, and after torturing people that are close to me with texts, emails, random questions, and passionate comments in all those moments I felt excited, doubtful, excited again, tired, and excited again when sitting in front of the laptop and writing this workbook. While some people say that writing a book takes a village, I would like to say that, for me, writing a book takes a village of people to see and trust my work as a clinician. I want to take a couple of moments to acknowledge that village of people!

There is a large international community that I feel very grateful to for being a source of knowledge and comradery, full of brilliant academicians, researchers, clinicians, and overall passionate people that want to make a difference in the world: The Association of Contextual Behavioral Science. Thank you for all what you do!!!!

There is also a group of people that always support me in all my endeavors: my family! Thank you tons to my mom Patricia, mi hermana Paolita, mi tia Sofia, mi tio Franklin, and my brother-in-law Marcelo, for telling me that this workbook looks good—even when you didn't fully get it—and yet, you always encourage me all the way!

Bazillion thanks to my adopted brother Russ, for seeing me as I am, seeing my work as it is, pushing me, cheering me, and always getting back to me despite having thousands of things to do!

Tons of thanks to Louise Gardner for putting her amazing artistic touch on this workbook with the illustrations!

I'm especially grateful to Maggie, my intake coordinator and personal boss, whose handy skills help me to make the most of every day at the office, my writing time, and my day-to-day tasks dealing with running a clinical practice.

I'm indebted to my mentor and lifelong friend Matt, for introducing me to ACT. I'm eternally thankful for our friendship, all the work we have done together, and your ongoing support finding my clinical expertise!

Tons of thanks to Jane, from JKP, for her guidance and support with this project! It was a treat to collaborate together on this manuscript!

I want to thank my friends Lucia, Simret, Geri, Ben, David, and Chris, for all your support with this project, tolerating long days of writing, hanging in there with my writing blocks, your patience with my middle-of-the-night notations, and the tasty vegan meals we shared together. You made this writing project possible while reminding me to keep my values at the front.

Finally, my heartiest thanks to the hundreds of children, teens, and parents I worked with over the years. All those thousands of hours we spent in my office, and outside in the community, practicing values-guided exposures, one after another, dancing with obsessions, and figuring out together what comes next have been an ongoing source of inspiration and a reminder that learning to live with fear, worries, and anxieties is a skill that can be cultivated and practiced every day to keep moving forward in life.

And of course, tons of gratitude to all the teens that were my consultants when working on this workbook. You rock!